8 Ways to Happiness from Wherever You Are

8 Ways
to
Happiness

FROM
WHEREVER
YOU ARE

DR. MARISSA PEI

NEW YORK

LONDON • NASHVILLE • MELBOURNE • VANCOUVER

8 Ways to Happiness

From Wherever You Are

Published in New York, New York, by Morgan James Publishing. Morgan James is a trademark of Morgan James, LLC. www.MorganJamesPublishing.com

The Morgan James Speakers Group can bring authors to your live event. For more information or to book an event visit The Morgan James Speakers Group at www.TheMorganJamesSpeakersGroup.com.

ISBN 9781683508557 paperback
ISBN 9781683508564 eBook
Library of Congress Control Number: 2017960677

Cover Design by:
Christopher Kirk
www.GFSstudio.com

Interior Design by:
Christopher Kirk
www.GFSstudio.com

Cover photo by Ken Rochon
Make-up by Dominique Lerma
Hair by Jerome Gillamac

In an effort to support local communities, raise awareness and funds, Morgan James Publishing donates a percentage of all book sales for the life of each book to Habitat for Humanity Peninsula and Greater Williamsburg.

Get involved today! Visit
www.MorganJamesBuilds.com

Praise for 8 Ways to Happiness

Wonderfully written! Easy and fun to read, it's packed with great insights. If you feel unhappy more than you'd like, this is exactly the right book. I am so glad you found it!

— **Neale Donald Walsch,**
New York Times Best-selling author of *Conversations with God*

I know strength. The kind of strength it takes to fight all the angles of adversity we face in life, as my dad gracefully role-modeled for me. Dr. Marissa has captured the essence of using inner strength and Universal fortitude to process the necessary and unavoidable pain in life. You can discover the undefeated champion within you, by using this book to guide you to your strongest self!

— **Laila Ali,**
4-time undefeated Boxing World Champion and daughter of the great Muhammad Ali

This book is self- help on steroids, a cross between I'm Ok You're Ok... you're Still OK and Don't Sweat the Small Stuff...AND the Big Stuff!" It's a book for anyone who is on antidepressants anti-anxiety medication who is still anxious depressed and now has side-effects on top of it!" Read it for long-lasting inside out relief!

—**David Hancock,**
Founder, Morgan James Publishing

People always ask me how I have managed to stay ageless since my role as Maryann on Gilligans island, and it's really not a big secret…I credit a positive attitude and a vision for happiness which is why I adore Dr. Marissa's book. *8 Ways to Happiness from Wherever You Are* captures the essence of what it takes to live in happiness 88% of the time. It's not only inspirational it's motivational practical and perfect to have especially if you ever get stuck on a desert island!

—Dawn Wells,
Actress and Author of *What would Maryann do?: A Guide to Life*

The book you hold in your hands is a trustworthy guide to expanding inner happiness. Marissa Pei shares not only the work she has done with her clients, but the work she has done within herself, the challenges she has personally, victoriously walked through. Wise are those readers who allow her to give them a "peace" of her mind… *8 Ways to Happiness* awakens us to the fundamental happiness that is the birthright of every human being. I encourage you to read these pages slowly, take their practices to heart, and watch how they will bless your life."

— Michael Bernard Beckwith,
Global Thought Leader, Oprah Super Soul 100 List of Awakened Leaders,
Founder of renowned Agape International Spiritual Center

8 Ways to Happiness is a roadmap for fulfillment and engaged living that I consider a must read. Especially in today's volatile times, Dr. Marissa Pei has found answers. She provides practical help, coupled with sharp writing and a keen sense of humor. I would suggest this book as a must read for every person I know."

—Cheryl Snapp Conner,
CEO, speaker, Forbes.com columnist and author of *Beyond PR: Communicate Like a Champ in the Digital Age.*

The greatest gift we can give ourselves is to re-discover our brilliance and our authentic selves; this book offers us the path. Dr. Marissa's vibrant words and pages are laced with humor, wisdom and challenge. She claims, 'You can rise above everything that stands in your way,' and with this brilliant work your dreams are sure to become reality. Dive in and soar!"

—Werner Berger
Guinness World Records holder, Corporate Leadership Consultant, Best Selling Author and Adventurer

"Warning: Once you start reading the first few pages, you may not be able to put *8 Ways to Happiness* down . . . even if you are already vibrantly happy. You may even skim the index breathlessly yearning to devour the content. Are you "waiting" for the next fabulous event in your life to be the thing that will finally make you happy? There is a sad moment when we become "grown ups" and realize that our childhood dream of wishing upon a star to get what we want is just not going to happen. At that point, we are faced with two choices: live the rest of your life feeling like others are living the life you were meant to live, OR live the rest of your life living the life you were meant to live. Happiness is the key to living the life that you "Wished Upon a Star" for and this is the book that will make that wish come true!

—Erin Saxton
Multi Emmy Nominated Producer for *Barbara Walters* and *The View*

"Entertaining and enjoyable! This book is filled with easy follow steps that are accessible to everyone that will have happiness beating a path to your door."

—Dan "Nitro" Clark
Former NFL player and star of the American Gladiators and bestselling author of *F Dying*

"In the Mind-Body-Spirit category many new titles issue each year, but few deliver the passion, humor, courage, and insight Dr. Marissa Pei offers her readers. Each person will find themselves in this book, regardless of the spiritual experience and self-knowledge they believe they already possess. *8 Ways to Happiness from Wherever You Are* is a tangible gift for those seeking a compassionate and honest voice to guide them down their path, a set of actionable tools to support them on their way, and the soft light of inner serenity waiting for them at the end."

—Karen Stuth,
Founder and Owner, *Satiama Publishing* and *Satiama Writers Resource*

"After being a guest on Dr. Marissa's talk radio/TV show we became very good friends and I am so happy to endorse her beautiful book *8 Ways to Happiness from Wherever You Are*. We all go through pain in life but every experience has meanings and it's progress to discover yourself and to find a happier road.

I express my emotions thru music, it's like a mirror and spreading light…
I believe that by reading this book, you'll receive light…and feel support
and love for your soul quest.
She is the messenger."

—Keiko Matsui,
Composer, Contemporary Jazz Pianist, Humanitarian

Dr. Marissa the Happiness DOCTOR's book is a vital "MUST READ"
for leaders everywhere to move from miserable to happy! As head of the
1 ranked entrepreneur institution serving 147 nations for thirty years
and home of record-breaking reads like *Chicken Soup, Rich Dad, Men are
from Mars, Three Feet From Gold, You Were Born Rich, Think & Grow Rich
For WOMEN, and THE SECRET's* Lisa Nichols' million dollar advance
for NO MATTER WHAT - *8 Ways to Happiness From Wherever You Are*
is NEXT!

—Berny Dohrmann
Founder CEO SPACE International

Have ever experienced meeting someone for the first time and felt like
you have known them forever? That's exactly how I felt when I met Dr.
Marissa Pei for the first time; it was love and friendship at first sight.…
You instantly smile at her quirky fashion, you are intrigued with her
wisdom and when she steps on the stage she entertains you, educates you
and does it with humor and heart. Her book will make you laugh, give
you the keys to living a joyful life and you will discover the secret behind
breaking through your fears to find your life purpose. If you are stuck and
need guidance to move forward with commitment, don't hesitate, take
the leap and read her book!

—Shea Vaughn,
Co-Founder/CEO, Women's Broadcast Television Network: Creator/CEO
SheaNetics®

"I've had the pleasure of watching Dr. Marissa grow unfold and expand
into the bright light that she is… and this book *8 Ways to Happiness from
Wherever You Are* is a roadmap to that journey."

—Adam Markel,
Bestselling Author of *Pivot: The Art & Science of Reinventing Your Career and Life*

What a great book to help those who feel a bit "stuck" in old habitual patterns of the mind. The principles Dr. Marissa lays out in 8 Ways to Happiness are easy to understand and grasp. If you're ready to move forward in life and break the broken record that stuck minds often play, then please read this book! In the words of Michael Jackson, "If you want to make the world a better place, take a look at yourself and then make the change."

—September Dohrman,
President and CEO of CEO Space International, Inc. and Forbes rated Must Attend Business Conference

"Dr. Marissa affectionately known as the Asian Oprah dispels the adage that happiness is fleeting. If you let her give you a peace of her mind and her heart, and practice using her balance tools, you too can be happy most of the time!"

—Greg Reid,
Author - *Think and Grow Rich* series

"*8 Ways to Happiness from Wherever You Are* exercises your mind, body and soul. It is like having a personal mentor whispering in your ear, one who helps you bring your choices and options into focus. Dr. Marissa gives you the opportunity to take your consciousness and life from woe is me to WOW, **I AM**! If you're ready for the Big Wave, get this book and jump into the life you have always wanted."

—Heshie Segal,
Speaker, Best-selling author, Founder of Kids Better World, and the Global Clean Water Movement, Puritii for Humanity

It's not about how many times you get knocked out, it's about how many times you get up and fight back! Dr. Marissa Pei gives great insight for anyone looking to understand the true meaning of life.

—Jeffrey Hayzlett,
Primetime TV & Podcast Host, Guest Celebrity Judge on NBC's Celebrity Apprentice, Speaker, Author and Part-Time Cowboy "Dr Marissa,

You've slapped me towards my Happiness with such LOVE! Sharing with you in the last month a surprise divorce and a serious car accident, I was feeling very hopeless. Reading and re-reading your truthful yet humorous book snapped me to HOPE again! *8 Ways to Happiness* will be on the best

seller list and the only gift I give to family and friends! You are my angel!
I could write much more but why! Read your book!
Feel the love"

—Marji Bordeaux,
Intellectual Property Patent and Trademark Consultant

"When Dr. Marissa taught at my Extreme Leadership Experience, she wowed the audience with her unique combination of energizing inspiration and down-to-earth style. *8 Ways to Happiness* embodies the essence of her message and approach. It's like having a personal motivational partner on your life's journey, helping you to make the right choices every step of the way. Read and be happy!"

—Steve Farber,
Author, *The Radical Leap*, *The Radical Edge* and *Greater Than Yourself*; Founder, The Extreme Leadership Institute

To my beloved dad who is on the other side…still being the one that I always knew I could fall back into, and the best human example of unconditional love that I have experienced in this lifetime.

To my 9th grade English teacher who said I was a horrible writer…
thanks for giving me a way out of writer's block!
Finally, to all of you out there who think that you're not good enough…
because you already are.

Table of Contents

Foreword

As human beings, we have a sense of entitlement where happiness is concerned and for good reason: happiness is our true nature. Happiness has been explored across all spiritual traditions, by philosophers, psychologists and even science. Nevertheless, most human beings don't realize that the soulware for happiness was encrypted within us the moment we came into existence. Happiness is the basic nature of life itself. And, as His Holiness the Dalai Lama reminds us, "Happiness is the highest form of health."

Activating our happiness soulware is a choice, a conscious decision to be grateful for one's life, including all the challenges and opportunities that come into our experience for our growth, unfoldment, healing, and spiritual evolutionary progress. As Marissa wisely underscores, in our search for happiness, it is helpful to become clear about whether or not we are pursuing authentic happiness or its shadow: pseudo pleasure. Our world is flooded with happiness vendors, be it in the form of books, workshops, or healing modalities. And yet happiness cannot be forced upon us nor can we force it upon others. Each of us must give our consent to being happy. And when we download our happiness soulware, we activate the deep roots of joy within the human spirit that transcend external conditions.

The human ego thrives on hearing that the path of transformation doesn't involve work or discipline. For example, the inspiration that comes from reading spiritual books is easier to assimilate than the per-spiration of actual practice of universal spiritual principles. When we consciously choose to cultivate happiness from the inside out, it is an expression of our growing spiritual maturity, because we realize we are co-creators of our destiny.

If you want to be happy, welcome challenges! Let them interrupt your familiar mindscape. Make friends with them, because within you is all that you require to work with them skillfully. Consider using this won-derful aspiration of Buddhist teacher Sylvia Boorstein: "May I meet this moment fully. May I meet it as a friend."

The book you hold in your hands is a trustworthy guide to expanding inner happiness. Marissa Pei shares not only the work she has done with her clients, but the work she has done within herself, and the challenges she has personally, victoriously walked through. Wise are those readers who allow her to give them a "peace" of her mind. Most importantly, *8 Ways to Happiness* awakens us to the fundamental happiness that is the birthright of every human being. I encourage you to read these pages slowly, take their practices to heart, and watch how they will bless your life.

Michael Bernard Beckwith
Agape International Spiritual Center
December 2017

Preface

So why do I get to give advice? Well, the title of my weekly syndicated talk radio show is ***Take My Advice, I'm Not Using It: Get Balanced with Dr. Marissa!*** And truth be told, I have actually used my own advice to transform my life. I suffered for decades, a seething bitter cauldron of hateful tears towards a mom that beat me as a child and a 'wasband' that cheated on me, and then cheated me out of a lot of money in an ugly divorce. On the outside, I looked like I was adjusting pretty well, but on the inside, it was dark and ugly and the 'infection' was starting to seep out and the odor was deadly. For years I thought I was unique in my pain and suffering. But I have found that I am not alone; it seems the price of admission as a human being is the unavoidable touchstone called pain. And despite what we watched on the TV show, 'Leave it to Beaver", up to 70% of us grow up in dysfunctional homes according to psychological research. Oprah claims it's 8 out of 10 homes, and since I was introduced to her by my honorable moniker "the Asian Oprah," I will agree with her! So, there are many, many people walking around with painful pasts that can be hidden or suppressed or repressed or denied or ignored for decades until it boils over… usually resulting in mid-life crisis, ill health, or broken relationships.

When I speak on stage, I like to use this analogy—that past pain in your life is like trash in a garbage disposal truck. Painful events have happened to you through no fault of your own but you can't change it, so

'Oh well just ignore it, pull yourself up by your bootstraps and get over it' reactions end up being pressurized by the garbage truck's automated arm that comes down and crushes the past pain, which, if you keep pushing down long enough and hard enough, turns into liquid, and then eventually into gas. So, in short, what you don't deal with will eventually come back and deal with you! And the funny, not so funny, part of that gas that you're leaking is that you can't smell it, but EVERYBODY around you can! You may think that you are successfully hiding your pain, but you're not. You think that you are more effective than you actually are. You scream at the top of your lungs, "I'm NOT ANGRY"! You are perplexed when people whisper that you are mean, unkind, scattered, anxious, obnoxious, angry, a downer, but you think you are fabulous. All of these are symptoms of leaking gas!

As an organizational psychologist, I get called in to do Executive Coaching with individuals that are leaking gas; technically brilliant, emotionally and interpersonally challenged individuals who have been able to hold it together for years, but are now coming undone. 88% of my clients are leaking gas from past pain. The good news is, there is a solution, and you do not have to stay plugged up any longer. And the best news is that it will not take you a lifetime of therapy, of constantly reliving the pain, nor will it require drugs with harmful side effects or a lobotomy to be happy again. Thanks to my own painful past, and working with this Balance Healing process I've used on myself and thousands of clients, I know there are 8 ways to happiness from wherever you are now!

This book is a Handbook for Happiness just for you. If you are stuck in Loneliness, there is a hand up with Hope. If you are swimming in the grief of Loss, there is a lifesaver of Faith within your reach. If your heart has been broken, there is a non-crazy glue called Love. If you are burning from Hatred, there is an ice-cold drink called Forgiveness. If you are sinking from Shame, there is a lift called Dignity you can step into. If you are paralyzed in Fear, there is a power called Freedom. If you are in pain from Perfectionism, there is relief with Joy. And if you are constricted from trying to control everything and everyone, let go into Happiness, 88% of the time.

Why 88%? Well, I'm Chinese, and in Mandarin the number 8 is a homonym for good fortune, so you'll see this lucky number used a lot in my work and in my writing. It's also not 100% happy because we need contrast; you can't know happiness if there aren't some points of unhappiness to contrast with, and through which we expand. So if you are unhappy right now, that's a GREAT thing. It has brought you to this book and now I get to splatter Hope and Happiness on to you! And warning… there are no side effects to this treatment, no after-taste, no increased thoughts of suicide and no decrease in libido. You do need to read, identify, cry, laugh, claim, see, decide, learn, practice and heal.

The format of the book starts each chapter with a Sound Familiar? section that helps you identify what you're feeling with statements and real vignettes so that you know that I know what you're going through. Then I give you a "Peace of My Mind and Heart" theory where we identify the BS (Belief Systems) and voices in our heads that keep us stuck. We replace them with new Belief Systems in a Foundation Peace so that you can stop marinating in unhappiness. Finally, there's Learning in Action, where I give you Balance Tools like the Power of Choice to practice strengthening your Balanced Centered Self muscle so you get out of your past pain and your future fear to claim your birthright, which is to be In Joy and Enjoy this thing called life. You are Loving, Loveable, Loved, and wrapped in a warm blanket of Worthiness…and I am excited to take this journey back to who you really are with you.

You are a child of the universe,
no less than the trees and the stars; you have a right to be here.
And whether or not it is clear to you,
no doubt the universe is unfolding as it should.

Therefore, be at peace with God,
whatever you conceive Him to be,
and whatever your labors and aspirations,
in the noisy confusion of life keep peace with your soul.

With all its sham, drudgery, and broken dreams,
it is still a beautiful world.
Be cheerful.
Strive to be happy.

Max Ehrmann, Desiderata, Copyright, 1952.

Introduction

If you are a happy person 88% of the time, stop reading. This book is only for folks who are wondering why they are not happy, wondering if they'll ever be happy or know someone who is in that boat. This is a book for people like me who have followed the rules, lived a life as prescribed by Snow White and Cinderella, and are wondering where 'happily ever after' went. I worked hard. I made myself as beautiful as I could. I married a frog in hopes that he would turn into a prince. Not only did he not transform himself, but he also hopped away with the riches in my pumpkin chariot and with my crystal slipper. Was that my prince? Is there a prince? Do I want a prince? Do I truly need someone to complete me? I wanted someone to take my breath away…and he did…and I nearly suffocated!

And then there are those of us who live a life called the "American Dream" and are wondering why we are waking up in the middle of an American Nightmare! I went to school and got good grades. Chose a lucrative career. Worked hard. Got promoted. Earned respect. Volunteered. Was a nice boss. Good team player. Nice house. Nice car. Nice vacations. So why am I not happy? Because I hate my job, lost my job, lost my marriage, lost my health, lost my kids, lost hope, and came to the conclusion that Happiness is Fleeting or Over-rated or Never to be Found.

This book is especially written for high achievement-oriented, perfectionistic, hard-working, successful on the outside, and control freaks on the inside who are exhausted, tired and frustrated…just like me! So if you are tired of being tired… and want to find your way back into Hope and Happiness 88% of the time… this book is for you.

When there is no enemy within, the enemies outside cannot hurt you.
-African Proverb

CHAPTER 1

Out of Loneliness...into Hope

L et's get in the mood for this chapter.

Take a deep breath, close your eyes and think of the last time you felt lonely.

Take a deep breath and follow it into your heart.

Still your mind and let yourself feel sad.

It's time to face the underlying loneliness that we all feel.

If you are feeling hopeless, that's okay. That's good.

Think of the last time you felt like it was you against the world.

Let your deepest darkest fears bubble up right now.

It's okay, you are not alone, but it's time to recognize that deep place inside you that you don't want to face.

We are going to 'go there' together now and find a way out of that low-grade sense of separation that keeps us from happiness.

CHECK ALL THAT APPLY:

- ❑ I sit in a dark room.
- ❑ Dark thoughts cross my mind.
- ❑ No one cares.
- ❑ I am worthless.

- ❑ I am tired.
- ❑ No one will ever love me.
- ❑ I don't belong.
- ❑ I hate being alone but can't stand being surrounded.
- ❑ I hate people.
- ❑ I hate myself.
- ❑ I feel so empty inside.
- ❑ I will live and die alone.
- ❑ I am done.
- ❑ I'm alone. Again. Of course.
- ❑ A chipmunk sings in the background, "Lonely, I am so lonely." How pathetic am I?
- ❑ No one knows my emptiness, my loneliness, my pain.
- ❑ All alone again.

Sound Familiar?

If you've checked more than half, I know how you feel…

Sarah: "There is a black hole in my life. I am afraid to feel lonely, to feel alone, to feel sad, to feel anything deep at all because if I go into that black hole I am afraid I will never find my way back out. That I will fall and fall and there will be no bottom. That if I do land, I will die broken. Into a million pieces. Worse than Humpty Dumpty because nothing and no one will be able to put me together again. So, I don't go there. I don't recognize the hole. I avoid it at all costs."

Chris: "I see people sitting all around me, and they are laughing and enjoying each other, and there is a glass cake cover that traps me away from them. I stand in the center, in my armor of loneliness, rusting from the heavy, black tears that sit inside, unshed."

Sarah is not alone. Chris is not alone. Every single person I've coached who has experienced trauma in their life, especially early on, can identify with this big black hole that yawns ominously in front of us. This is the dark power of loneliness. This is the power of depression. This is the power of past pain. I ran from that hole for over a decade. I couldn't find relief in denial. The darkness became harder to ignore. I woke up with it. And I couldn't fall asleep for fear of falling into it. I started trying to fill the hole with people or places or things.... anything to stop the big black yawning horrifically empty dark painful hole from swallowing me into oblivion.

And loneliness breeds emptiness. So, we try to fill that empty void by turning to temporary fillers, many of which have terrible side-effects and consequences.

> *Tom*: "I know there's something wrong with me. I don't want to be around people, but at the same time I hate being alone. All of my marriages end with me sitting alone with my computer. Chat rooms helped for a little while, but they are not true connections. I crave connection and then at the same time, I am terrified or disgusted by it. Just leave me alone and let me play my computer games."

> *Deborah*: "I eat to try to fill up my empty hole of meaninglessness. I also smoke to fill it and it's such a disgusting habit that it automatically isolates me from others. Which is fine, I don't need people... do I? Drinking also helps; I feel really good at that first 'ahhhh.' But after two DUI's I can't afford to fill that way anymore."

Loneliness... Discomfort... Anxiety... Apathy... Numb... Dead and Alive. Quick, give me something so I don't have to sit in the bottomless despair of muck. When the streetcar named Loneliness attacks, I turn to a numbing aid: food, alcohol, and drugs from the pharmacy or from a dealer, cigarettes, computer games, finishing a 12-hour read of books at one sitting, internet dating sites, chat rooms...anything to soothe that dark ugly empty place. Anything to turn myself away from myself. Anything to fill the bottomless hole of discomfort with an illusory pseudo-filling substance. I know that feeling well.

Numbing through food quickly becomes expensive as it requires a whole new wardrobe of larger-sized clothes. Emotionally, there is a dramatic increase in "fat and ugly" attacks. Alcohol has legal ramifications, especially if there is a proclivity towards blackouts and/or DUI's. Drugs have similar consequences. Cigarettes are now more expensive and have a pretty bad after-taste. Computer games and reading, while not dangerous, are time-stealers and you might find that your job gets in the way. Internet dating and chat rooms are a cross between games and blackouts. Denial fails. Numbing fails. Now what?

Let Me Give You A "Peace" of My Mind

There is an end to the feeling. You will not fall forever. I promise. But you have to decide whether you want to listen to the truth or live in the lies.

Here are the Lies:

- No one cares.
- I am worthless.
- No one will ever love me.
- I will never be good enough.
- It's pointless.
- I don't belong.
- I will die without ever knowing true love.
- No one will care when I am gone.
- I can't make anyone happy.
- I will live alone.
- I will die alone.
- No one knows my emptiness, my loneliness, my pain.

Loneliness is self-imposed. Its strength is founded in the lie of separation. Somewhere along the line, we bought into the idea that we were separate from the Universe, God, the eternal energy of love, light, good in the Universe, and from each other. We grew to believe that we are not connected with something greater than ourselves. That we are alone and disconnected and that we deserve to be isolated. That we have to earn our relationships by doing what others or the commandments want. That there is a price to pay to be connected anywhere, to anyone. The potency of the lie stems from win or lose, better than worse than. So, we judge people in relation to ourselves and each other, and spend our lives in this confusing dance of I want you, I don't want you, I want to be in love, I don't need love, I am enough, I am not enough, I'm better than you, I'm worse than you, I am a piece of 'shiitake', I am hot 'shiitake'.

It's not just a vicious circle, it's a vicious swing, and it is exhausting. No wonder we think it's just better to move away to a deserted island. I'll be the one person to prove the philosopher wrong; I can be an island! My powerful self-protective façade tells me I don't need or want anyone, that I am meant to be and want to be alone. That I am the one exception to the rule of social animal, that I was not made normal, that I don't have the desire nor need to be connected. That I am alone. These are the ultimate lies that will keep us marinating and "ruin-ading" in loneliness. So, what's the solution? What's the way out of loneliness into hope and happiness?

Foundation Peace: Choose Your Truth

Human beings have a secret weapon to use for Happiness 88% of the time. What is it? It's called the Super Power of CHOICE! Einstein says that the most important question that a human being has to answer is "Is this a Friendly Universe?" If you CHOOSE to believe that the Universe is NOT Friendly, it's going to be a LONG HAUL! You're always going to be looking over your shoulder to see who's going to hurt you, take from you, lie to you, break your trust, break your heart, steal from you. No matter what good happens you'll be waiting with bated breath for that 'other shoe to drop.' That will lead to isolation, holding back, holding people away and unhappy LONELINESS!!

On the other hand, you could CHOOSE another Truth—that the Universe is Friendly and conspiring on your behalf for more goodness, more love, more joy, and well-being, which is the foundation of life. Is there proof that this is true? Well, that depends on where you look.

I hear some of you asking, "But if the Universe is friendly, then why is there so much tragedy, so much killing, rape, and wrong in this world? It is NOT a Friendly Universe." BUT remember, the Balance tool is Choice. I can choose to focus on what I hear in the news (CNN-Constantly Negative News that 'leads if it bleeds') OR I can recognize that news producers CHOOSE what they want to put on the air, and select one from hundreds of thousands of things that are occurring in any one minute around the world. That's why the media is sometimes called a Weapon of Mass Distraction! There are many more positive news bites that never make it in front of us.

So it's up to you whether you are led by the morning news with messages of violence, lack, and limitation that are used to keep us in Fear and Hate and Blaming each other, or whether you CHOOSE to start your day with the truth. Borrowing from my teachers Esther and Abraham Hicks, "Well-being abounds on the planet, and we don't have to work hard to make that happen. The planets are in harmonious balance without us trying to control gravitational pull, that our bodies digest food and breathe without us turning a switch on. That we see evidence of well-being everywhere, including in the incredible occurrence that there is not one grain of sand or blade of grass or butterfly pattern or leaf or snowflake that is alike another." No accidents in that! So, every time I hear bad news I go looking for good news, and I always find it. There are billions of people doing beautiful things on the planet and I am so grateful that in my small way on my talk radio show I get to highlight a few so that I practice what I teach! I choose to know that the Friendly Universe is holding your and my hand. The Power that created all that is alive is always here waiting for us to connect with it.

The truth is that you are not alone no matter what your feelings, ego, and the liar in your head says. Finding the bottom of that deep dark hole begins with the decision to choose to believe. The name or theology or religion is not required and not necessary at this juncture. All we need to believe is that there is a Power that created the beauty and magnificence called Life. That Wonder is the hand you hold as you find the bottom of that big black hole. There is a Power of Good and a Power of Light that is always waiting for us to dance with. Like electricity, you can just plug yourself in. We are not alone. But it starts with our CHOICE to Choose to believe.

I was lucky. I actually had a Voice tell me so. I will never forget that day—February 22, 2009. I had been church shopping and one day I found myself sitting in the meditation portion of the service prior to hearing the founder of the Agape International Spiritual Center, Michael Bernard Beckwith, speak. A little aside to the kind of person I am, I was actually asked 5 years prior if I'd ever been to Agape, because apparently, I resembled the tone of the place; and as stubborn and bull-headed as I am, if you tell me I need to go do something or go somewhere, it will take me another 5 years to follow direction! Now back to the story… I was not a meditator at the time, so I was just listening to people cough and clear their throat around me when about 8 minutes in I felt a Presence move behind me, kind of like Batman on Hollywood Boulevard with a large wingspan and high black platform shoes. It/He/She tapped me on the shoulder and said, "Darlin', you can church-shop all you want and have fun with it, but know that I've always been here waiting for you to turn around and dance with me." I broke down. Tears of relief ran down my face as I realized I was Home. I wasn't alone, and I could stop running away from others and myself. I have never been alone or broken. I am a spiritual being having a human experience, and I am going to juice every bit of time I have on this Planet. I don't have to be alone. I choose to be connected to a Powerful Friendly Universe who I affectionately call my UPS Man, my Universal Power Source, and He delivers every morning when I pray and meditate.

You may be reading and thinking, "This sounds like religion and I'm too smart for that." I am actually 'allergic' to religion myself, so I am definitely not advocating a "one way to heaven" message here. However, I will ask you—whatever your BS (Belief System) is right now—is it working for you?! If it is, that's fabulous and I am truly happy for you and you don't need to read any further. However, most of the people

I meet are not having much luck feeling happy with their BS, so this book is for them. I love the expression from *The Spirituality of Imperfection by* Ernest Kurtz and Katherine Ketcham that *"Religion is for people who are afraid of going to **hell**; **spirituality** is for those who have already been there!"* I know that religion did not work for me, and, at the other extreme, having no belief in anything, also intensified my Loneliness and Hopelessness. Turning around that day to reconnect and dance with that Power removed the fear of that black hole once and for all. Now the hole is still there, and I do still dip into it occasionally when I am having a fat and ugly attack, but I know how to balance and move back into the Light of Hope. 88% of the time I am dancing around it and helping others by shining my flashlight so they can see their way out. I choose to be helped out of my Loneliness pit, and to help others with that lift up as well. Next are some Balance tools I've created that are useful for staying out of the Hole.

Learning in Action with Balance Tools

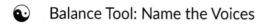 ### Balance Tool: Name the Voices

Most of us try to push away the darkness of loneliness until we can't escape. Then we fall in, and then it becomes very difficult to climb out… and then we lose hope in life. I see many clients when they are in that "mid-life crisis" time of their life. I've renamed it to "mid-life opportunity" because the silver lining is that we get to renew our lease on life by taking back control of our life car. When we are trapped in Loneliness and feeling hopeless we are primarily listening to one of the voices in our heads, the Sad one. She's the one who sits in the dark and is afraid to speak, play, or cry because she was beaten/hurt/shushed as a child whenever she tried to express herself. At some point, she takes over the controls of your life car and you are in a constant state of sadness, despair, grief, and listlessness. That overwhelming sense of loneliness described in the opening statements are constant chatter in the head from the Sad one. Give that sad little person inside of you a name. I call mine Sarah. Think about your pet name and use that. Now talk to your little sad one. For those of you who are saying, "Ahhh, this is Inner Child work," well it is, and more. Sarah isn't the only one in there. We have a whole committee in our heads who keep us stuck because they haven't progressed beyond past pain.

For many of us, the strongest voice yammering at us is the Critic. It's the voice that constantly tells you where you screwed up, the one that says, "you're so pathetic" when you start singing the "I'm so lonely" chipmunk song. It's the woulda-shoulda-coulda voice, the one that says, "You're never going to be good enough" and makes being alone a logical conclusion because "No one wants your company, you are a loser." I named my Critic Rose…and guess what my mother's name is? She did a great job criticizing me all my life with "You're fat, ugly, and clumsy." Now I am not saying that everything goes back to your relationship to your mom. But I do love the sayings, 'If it's not one thing, it's your mother,'; and there are two times in your life when you do not have mother issues — when you are born and when you die. Yes, many of us have mothers who were our first and strongest critic, so don't think you're alone. And then to add insult to injury, my internal critic, Rose, is now actually more powerful in my head than my mom's voice ever was. I've internalized all of the negative messages and even made up new ones.

Another voice in our heads is the Brat. I call mine Agnes. She is the voice that says, "Screw you, I don't need anyone, I don't like you anyways, I CAN live on a deserted island, I don't need people, I hate you, I can be happy with me myself, so LEAVE ME ALONE!"

In order to get out of loneliness and into hope, we have to start growing our Balanced Centered Selves (BCS) to soothe the Critical voice, the Bratty voice and the Sad, muffled voice. We all have a Balanced Centered Self who is named your true name. You can move yourself out of Loneliness into Hope by moving the Critic out of the driver's seat into the passenger seat before she/he drives us off a cliff, and strengthen practice and grow our Balanced Centered Selves. Then, and only then, will the Brat and the Sad, hopeless voice subside, and move to the back seat.

So what's the name of your Critic?

_____

_____

What's the name of your Sad One?

_____

_____

What's the name of your Brat?

_____

_____

What's the name of your Balanced Centered Self? (This is your true name)

_____

_____

Make sure you complete this naming exercise because we will be talking to each of your characters throughout the rest of this book.

☯ Balance Tool: Feel It Fully

One of the reasons we turn to food, drugs, alcohol, smoking, or something else to fill the emptiness is to try to avoid feeling the black hole fully, for fear of ending up like Humpty Dumpty. So, part of the movement out of Loneliness and into Hope is to make peace with our black hole. Instead of avoiding, stuffing, filling or covering it up, it's important to know that we can feel it fully and still be okay. Let your Balanced Centered Self guide you in the following Heart Opening exercise.

- Take some time right now, sit and write. Breathe in…. Exhale and release all the stories and the drama onto paper
- Describe your Loneliness

- Hold on and dive-in and give in to that horrific black hole of a feeling.
- Face the feeling head-on. Don't run or numb from it. Just sit in the discomfort.
- Put a timer on for 8 minutes.

Breathe it in.

Now explore it. That bottomless black chasm that most of us have, actually does have a bottom.

If you are beginning to feel panic or fear it's okay...this time, don't try to numb it away, just sit and breathe...in ... and out. In and out.

Breathe In with Light and in the out breath, release the darkness.

Breathe in Calm and out fear.

You are in the hole and you are okay.

And you have landed at the bottom... and you did not crash or break or shatter.

You are in a darkness that you have been afraid of for a long time, and I am here with you, holding a flashlight and your hand as we go exploring. There's nothing to be afraid of. It's not as black or as bottomless as you have been in fear of. It is actually more like the container you were in before you were delivered... warm and nutritious. Now let's go explore.

What is the texture of the bottom?

_____

_____

_____

What temperature is it?

_____

_____

_____

What color is it?

_____

_____

_____

What patterns does is have?

_____

_____

_____

Where do you feel it in your body?

_____

_____

_____

How does it feel in your body?

_____

_____

_____

Like pain.
Like sadness.
Gray.
Lack.
Hard.
Cold.
Warm.
Hot.

Describe it. Write it down if you like.

_____

_____

_____

And breathe. And cry. Hug yourself. Cry. Breathe. Jump up and down. Feel. Breathe. And feel. And breathe.

You will hear voices.

The Brat will say "This is stupid, it's not going to help, too 'woo woo,' I don't believe in therapy, I really don't need to deal with this."

The Critic will say, "Don't bother, it's not going to help, you're a lost cause, you might as well give it up, nothing you do will make you good enough, you deserve to be alone based on what you've said and done, you're hopeless, you're as bad as your mom said you were, you will be stuck in loneliness the rest of your life so you might as well end it now."

The Sad One will say "It hurts too much, stop please, I won't be able to survive this, I'm so hurt, I can't do this, I will get hurt again, I don't want to hope, there is no hope."

In the hole of Loneliness, we get an opportunity to connect with the Sad One and have your BCS Balanced Centered Self say "Hi, you can come out into the light now. I am here and you don't have to be alone or afraid anymore. You are a Precious Child of the Universe and your birthright is to come out of the darkness of Loneliness into the Light of Hope." Your Balanced Centered Self will take a breath and wrap her/his arms around the Sad one, the Brat, and the Critic, and say "I'm here, I got you, we are connected to the most powerful Light and Love in a Friendly Universe, we are not alone, and we never have to wallow in this loneliness again. The truth is we are precious, whole, and complete, imperfectly perfect with unique gifts, talents, and abilities to discover and develop and shine with for the rest of our lives."

Many of my clients feel remarkably better after one or two times of administering the Feel it Fully Balance Tool. If you are still afraid to go into the hole, that's okay… you may want to do this with a friend, a therapist, or a Life Balance coach who can encourage you to feel fully. And you don't have to do over and over again. When I work with my Life Balance clients, we actually go back one last time and shovel out the shiitake, plant the new seed from the Friendly Universe which we have been and always are an extension of. Once the Balanced Centered Self recognizes and plants the seed of who we really are, we put the shiitake back as fertilizer, because past pain will not get infected if we feel it fully, and tears are the disinfectant that keep our hearts soft.

After you finish this exercise you realize you have hit rock bottom and that you didn't free fall forever. And you are alive. And you are not alone. Now, jump into action to prove how valuable you are to yourself.

INTO PRACTICE:

☯ Balance Tool: Strengthening Your BCS

Are you ready for the truth? Jack Nicholson is asking… CAN YOU HANDLE THE TRUTH?! Your Balanced Centered Self will grow stronger as it replaces all the critical bratty and hopeless talk with the truth of who we are, and with Hope statements like:

- This feeling of loneliness will pass.
- It is ok to feel lonely.
- I am not condemned to be swallowed up by that empty feeling for the rest of my life.
- I may be alone physically but I am never alone spiritually.
- I am loved always, even when I don't feel like it.
- Just because I am alone doesn't mean I am not likable, lovable, worthy or enough.
- I can choose to do things when I am alone that I can't do in a crowd of chatter, such as compose, read, write, organize, pray, meditate, and play.
- The time I am alone is relatively small when I zoom out and look at my life as a whole.

- These feelings are just feelings, and they will subside.
- I will not die from my feelings.
- I choose not to act when my feelings are unsettling me…they will pass like the wind.
- Facts are walls and feelings are just a gust of wind and will pass.
- I can feel my feelings and then move on.
- Most of the time I can't even remember what I felt so sad/mad about last week.
- This too shall pass.

As you continue to separate truth from lies, the more light emits from your Staff of Truth, and you realize that the big black hole has a bottom. You will not fall endlessly and end up like Humpty Dumpty. You have the power to choose to believe in whatever you want—the lies or the truth—your choice.

These statements are the healing truth. But they have to be be practiced in order to be strengthened, to be stronger than the Critic and Brat voices that have been your predominant for most of your life.

☯ Balance Tool: Acting on Your Own Behalf

Loving yourself enough to take care of yourself involves acting on your own behalf, maybe not 100% of the time, because we're human and not perfect, but about 88% of the time. And it starts with that powerful weapon we are girded with called CHOICE. All of the bad habits that we have grown accustomed to using in order to fill that big black hole are no longer necessary. We get to exercise our new muscle called Acting on Our Own Behalf.

So…

- Choose not to go to the fridge.
- Choose not to surf the net for a stud surfer…aka on-line dating.
- Choose not to pick Jack Daniels, Johnny Walker, or any other guy on the street.
- Choose not to go to the pharmacy/dealer.
- Choose not to gamble.

- Choose not to smoke.
- Choose not to shop.
- Choose not to have meaningless sex.
- Choose not to take anything that will ultimately fail or just temporarily fill that hole that feels infinite but is more like a warm womb than a cold dark pit.

We can never know how finite the hole is if we numb, avoid, or run from it. And you are worth leaving the big black hole called Loneliness into the opening called Hope.

It won't be easy the first eight times. You will feel extremely uncomfortable. Your inner Brat will have a field day and shine its searchlight on the fridge, computer, medicine cabinet and/or liquor cabinet to try to convince you that "It's really not a big deal, that you need to feel better, that it's not an addiction to have 'just one', that no one is the boss of you, that you should be able to eat, drink, smoke, buy ANYTHING you feel like." The worst part is that if you do listen to the Brat and partake, the Critic will jump down your throat with "See, you are a piece of Shiitake, you can't keep promises to yourself, you're so weak, you can't even stop a bad habit that you know is terrible, you're so stupid, you will never amount to anything!" But if you hold on, and counter the back and forth crazy-making between the Brat and the Critic with Balanced Centered talk, it will get easier. I promise.

Strengthen your BCS and say, "This feeling to numb will pass whether we partake or not, I am worth breaking bad habits, I have a lot of creativity and happiness to share for the rest of my life, I don't have to be afraid, isolate, hide and wallow in Loneliness anymore. There is Hope for a New Day." The Brat and the Critic are waiting for Balanced Centered Self to take charge. The Critic in particular is very tired; it's been working overtime for so long! So, you can say "Have a seat, darlin', you have to be tired. Take a vacation, I got this."

In the next chapter, we will continue to understand this internal committee meeting and how we can have them come to order once and for all.

By sitting with the feeling and choosing to believe that we are not alone, and then choosing not to numb the darkness with people, places, and things, the huge scary yawning dark hole becomes more and more shallow, concrete, and finite. The more comfortable I learn to become with the bottom dark feeling of loneliness, the readier I am for the attack of loneliness, and the stronger I get to choose to act on my own behalf and let my Balanced Centered Self drive my life car. Sociologists say that it takes 28 days to break a bad habit. Likewise, it takes 28 days to learn a new good habit. They also say that 42 percent of statistics are made up on the spot. Sorry, my Brat just wrote that! Ignore her and start a great life habit that will keep you out of the Loneliness Hole.

I can let that feeling of loneliness come and then I can let that same feeling go. There are many resources that can help us with this. 12 step programs are my first recommendation because they are affordable, have a spiritual base, and a community to support you. But there are many systems out there to help; in fact, anyone who has found relief from numbing has a unique purpose to help others do the same because they know what you're going through. We can, hand in hand with a Power greater than ourselves and others, end the futile filling of our emptiness with smoke and mirrors and move Out of Loneliness into Hope.

Next, we are going to clean out the gaping hole in our heart that is dug when we lose someone we love… and fill it up with faith.

CHAPTER 2

Out of Loss... into Faith

Who do you miss? I miss my dad Dr. David Pei, my best friend Michael Main, my dog Destiny, my cousin George, my friend Dr. Jimi, my surrogate dad Dr. Carl McCraven, my Russian Jewish grandmother Anna Blum. All but two died before their time, unexpectedly from lymphoma, aids, stroke, heart attack, and cancer.

Yes, it hurts…

- When people die in a tragedy
- When people die before their time
- When people die unexpectedly
- When people die in old age
- When children die before their parents
- When people die from addiction
- When people die from suicide
- When babies die
- When parents die
- When family members die
- When friends die
- When pets die
- When people around the world die of starvation, of genocide, of war, of natural disasters
- When people die from freak accidents
- When people die from acts of war and terrorism.

19

Take a deep breath, close your eyes and allow yourself to remember who you miss.

Take a deep breath and follow it into your heart.

Still your mind and let yourself feel sad.

It's time to face the pain of loss that sometimes we stuff, hide, or marinade in to the point of paralysis.

We are going to 'go there' together now and find a way out of that aching pain that never seems to get better…from the pain of loss which keeps happiness fleeting.

CHECK ALL THAT APPLY:

- ❑ I can't stop missing you
- ❑ I really can't go on without you
- ❑ Why can't I stop crying?
- ❑ It wasn't his time
- ❑ It wasn't her time
- ❑ How could God let this happen?
- ❑ Why do the good ones go first?
- ❑ I didn't get to say goodbye
- ❑ I can't imagine life without him
- ❑ I would give anything to be the one to die
- ❑ I can't feel my heart anymore
- ❑ I want to die and be with her
- ❑ I want to end this feeling of heartbreak…please let me die
- ❑ Why should I bother anymore?
- ❑ Life is so unfair
- ❑ I don't care anymore
- ❑ Why should I care?
- ❑ If I died it would be a relief
- ❑ I can't take this anymore
- ❑ Please let me die to stop this pain
- ❑ Give me something to take this feeling away
- ❑ No one understands how I feel

❑ You can't possibly understand

❑ I will never be able to get past this pain

Sound Familiar?

If you've checked more than half, I feel you…

Losing someone you loved more than life itself is…well there really isn't a word that can capture the feeling of the deep black vacuum called loss. There is a model by Elizabeth Kubler Ross called the Stages of Death and Dying which describes the denial, anger, bargaining, depression and acceptance that individuals cycle through when there is loss, but even knowing that there is a theory doesn't guarantee that we don't get stuck in the happiness-robbing pain of loss.

If you are feeling the pain of loss as if it happened yesterday and it was far from yesterday, keep reading. If you are mad and confused and angry at God for the loss, keep reading. If you are numb and just waiting to die for the pain to go away, keep reading.

Let Me Give You A "Peace" of My Heart

Even when someone grows old and you know they aren't going to live forever, it still hurts. And aches. And feels like a giant yawn of bad breath that you have to escape from with any numbing substance that's nearby.

Judy: I loved my mom so much. She was my best friend. She could read my mind. She was my number one fan, and now she's gone, and I don't think I can live without her. It's been two years and I still wake up missing her and can't stop the tears. Nothing I say or do feels meaningful anymore.

My dad died way before his time. And in writing this I feel the tears come up. And it's okay. It's normal to miss someone who you knew loved you in a way that you've never been loved since. It's normal to want to see feel touch smell and talk to someone that you knew you could fall back into…that was my dad. Always there with a smile and a hug and a word and a 20-dollar bill. He went from near perfect health to waking up with bruises all over his body to collapsing in the bathroom to hundreds of tests to lymphoma to chemo to death in less than 8 months. Was I mad? Yes, at first. Was I sad? Yes, of course. Do I feel pain? Yes. Sometimes, when I think of how much he wanted grandkids and that he isn't physically here to hold them and play with them and laugh with them, I can feel bad. But do I suffer? I did for many years. I would make his death anniversary, his birthday, Father's Day, and Christmas as launch pads to wallow in the depths of missing, hurting, blaming and shaming so that I would have a lingering low-grade sense of loss all year long. The way we see death can hurt our chances of feeling happy 88% of the time.

> *Stacy*: "One day I was talking to her on the phone, and then next day she's been shot by her best friend's ex-husband. My beloved sister, gone, along with many others cut off in the prime of their life. I'm watching my parents die in front of me from grief, and I will never be able to be happy again. I have an ache that cannot be soothed and a hole so big you cannot help me up out of it again."

> *Travis*: "I used to believe in God. I grew up praying and trying to be a good person. And then too many bad things happen in the world, and then my brother was killed in a freak accident. He was the sweetest nicest most innocent person I knew. I should have been the one who died, not him. How could God let something like this happen? There is too much evil in this world to support the existence of a God. Life is a crapshoot and my brother lost…and I did too."

Unexpected loss through tragedy can bring us to our knees for the rest of our lives and stuck in unhappiness, if we let it. I was actually in the middle of the worst massacre in Orange County history in the Seal Beach Salon shooting in 2011. I watched all of the families of the eight victims who were gunned down by an angry out of control man in a custody battle grapple with the news that their sons, daughter, mother, wife, husband, grandmother were laying on the ground with bullet wounds…not knowing if they were dead or alive until 24 hours after the notification, and then told that they were dead. I wrote about the experience and the *Orange County Register* ran my account of what it was like witnessing the naked pain of loss from the front row seat in the library. Here's an excerpt:

> We were asked by the police not to talk about the case with the press. This is not about the case. This is about walking through the pain of tragedy, and sharing it to help myself and others to heal.
>
> Wednesday, I was sequestered in the Seal Beach library for six hours after the shooting tragedy at the salon. I write and talk and teach about Life Balance for a living. I am having to practice what I teach.
>
> The hardest part was waiting for word, not knowing who was actually dead, praying desperately with hope that the one in the hospital was theirs. I understand that because of the process, great care had to be taken in the investigation, but the not knowing was taking its emotional toll. My heart was broken the most when after one of the "We don't know anything yet" announcements came from the police, an older gentleman who was alone and shaking asked, "When will I know about my wife?" She was the 70-year-old woman getting her hair done.
>
> The grief counselors passed around helpful paperwork that hopefully will be useful later; no one was in the mood to read. I listened to the anger at the senselessness; the anger that this should have been prevented; the anger that they knew this was going to happen, that there were warning signs; the anger that the system doesn't work; the overwhelming sadness of loss; the bewilderment that this can't be happening, the "I can't believe this is happening" over and over again.
>
> I knew not to use any of my motivational phrases now, that "this too shall pass" and that "everything happens for a reason" was not going to be helpful. But to hold someone who is hurt-

ing from getting a piece of their heart cut out, and just say I am sorry, to let them lean on you, to tell them that their mom's energy is still here comforting them, and that she will always be in their heart, and that memories are reliving the love, and that allowing yourself to cry and feel and fall into those around you who love you, and to not be afraid to hurt when there is support, and to be strong when the children need holding… that is how we are going to get through this.

To engage in an argument about gun control, to blame politics, to blame the Universe is not…

That whatever you are feeling is okay, that it is okay to hurt, that you are loved, that even though it doesn't feel like it now, there is a bottom of love to break your fall, that in time and love you will heal, but for right now, just cry. Tears are the disinfectant that keeps your heart pure and open. I am comforted by my own words…

What can we do? Pray for comfort to our families. Pray for peace. Tell everyone who is important to you and you are important to them that you love them. Forgive anyone that you aren't loving right now. Hug all day. And then we will heal, one day at a time.

—By ORANGE COUNTY REGISTER October 14, 2011 at 4:50 pm

As I wrote, there were trained 'Grief Counselors' who walked around with pamphlets that outlined the stages of death and dying and how to feel better. The families were in absolutely no shape or place to read or talk to a stranger no matter how trained they were. When tragedy strikes, there is no way to lessen the pain. But there is a way to traverse pain so that it does not permanently impact life happiness.

Past pain from loss of loved ones can get stuck in our intellectual, physical, emotional, and spiritual pores. And what you don't deal with will eventually come back and deal with you! Depression is unprocessed pain, or sadness on steroids. When we lose loved ones, our ability to heal from loss is dependent on processing through that pain fully and completely, without avoiding or denying or hiding or stuffing or glossing or justifying or blaming or burying. So, are you ready to heal the pain of loss? Pain is mandatory, yes, but Suffering is optional. If you're ready to embrace the pain of loss and ease back out into Faith, keep reading. Let's start with our BS (Belief Systems) clogging our mind and then balance out with exercises to help heal our hearts.

Let Me Give You A "Peace" of My Mind

Why do we suffer when we lose people we love? Why do we blame an angry vengeful uncaring God when tragedy strikes? Why do we lose faith in the goodness of life, ourselves and others? Somewhere along the line, we think that we are all entitled to a long fruitful life, and even live forever because even when our loved ones die of 'old age' we are still consumed with grief. We take it personally that if life was fair, we would all live to 100 in good health and die in our sleep…and so anything other than that means we are being picked on. We are not supposed to get sick, we are not supposed to lose loved ones, we are supposed to be awarded with an easy life as long as we are good people and follow the 10 commandments, go to church and volunteer in the community. So how is that BS (Belief System) working for you? As another one of my teachers, and past guest Neale Donald Walsh says in his book, "What God Said," "You think you are being terrorized by other people but in truth you are being terrorized by your own beliefs." What if we chose a different truth to awaken to in life?

Foundation Peace: Choose Your Truth

Here are the Belief Systems (BS) that keep us suffering when we lose people we love.

- They are gone forever.
- They should have lived longer.
- I cannot live without them.

- God is unfair and cruel to take them so early.
- There must not be a God for evil people to live and good people die.
- Evil takes everything good from me.
- I am supposed to live a full life into my 90's to be fulfilled and anyone that dies before that has failed.
- If we obey the commandments, be a good person, do our job, raise our families, be responsible, be of good cheer no matter the circumstances, then we will have lived a good life in preparation for a better life in heaven, and tragedy should leave us alone.
- When someone does die tragically, then we are being punished.
- When they are taken in the prime of their life, then they are cheated and we are cheated.

These Belief Systems lead to feelings of hopelessness, sadness, depression, confusion, apprehension, anxiety, doom, why bother, blame, anger, resentment, and hate.

What if there was another way to see life?

What if we CHOOSE to believe instead…

- Life is Eternal, and there is a chapter called Human Being that has a start called birth and an end called death.
- That death is just a transition into another chapter that could be Heaven or something else. From the reports of those who have crossed and returned, the majority say that it is a bright light place and full of peaceful feelings. Since they didn't get too far before they came back we don't know what the chapter really entails but we will, when it's our time. I'll choose to believe the word that is most used when folks cross to the other side for a second before returning…Peace.
- That when tragedy happens, when bad things happen to good people, it's not a punishment but an opportunity to have our hearts break wide open, to develop more qualities, to expand our ability to love and be compassionate and show kindness.
- What if life is just about having experiences…to love, to hold,

to lose, to laugh, to cry, to desire, to be disappointed, to celebrate, to grieve, to comfort, to serve, to create, to inspire, to build, to invent, to sculpt, to communicate, to fight, to resolve, to believe, to question, to achieve, to fail, to learn, to grow and expand…what if that is what life is all about, and the length of time isn't as important as the ability to experience fully.

• What if all of the circumstances that happen to and around us are to sculpt us into beautiful creations…that we start as blocks of precious marble that contain a unique, precious one of a kind piece of art…and that life is about discovering through creative chiseling that is sometimes a bit painful, who we are. And that our life's purpose is to carve out and unearth our unique gifts talents and abilities…and honing them with the time in this lifetime. What if tragedy has a role in helping us with that chiseling?

My favorite guests on my talk radio show are those who have gone through tragedy and found a purpose in helping, founding, promoting organizations that help ensure that those kinds of tragedies don't happen again. The Joyful Foundation founded by Erin Runnion, came out of her daughter's kidnapping and murder. Paul Wilson, husband of Christy Lynn Wilson, one of the eight people killed in my hometown in the Seal Beach salon shooting, used his pain to fight for legislation to limit gun permits to anyone involved in a custody battle.

Am I saying that tragedies happen by design to break our hearts open? That there is some puppeteer up in the sky orchestrating a mass chiseling of humans? Absolutely not. But as I established in the last chapter, I choose to believe in a Friendly Universe. I choose to believe that everything happens for my Divine and best good. I choose to believe that even when it hurts like a knife, when it feels like it's going to kill me, when the loss feels like it's going to go on forever, even when I don't think I can go on without them, even if I want to scream and blame and ask why and try to make sense out of the insensible…I can feel all of it and then choose a different future for myself. I can choose to know that this horrific feeling is temporary, that this anguish will pass with time and a choice to love and balance. In time, I will be able to see the good that came out of the tragedy, the loss, as the expression says, "A year knows what a day doesn't".

When I am faced with loss it ignites in me a choice, to be grateful every day for the people in my life, for however long that may be. Loss will not rob me of feeling or being fully alive. There doesn't have to be a blanket of heaviness just because someone has transitioned on to another time and space when I choose to believe that this thing called life is just one of many chapters in the Eternal. Do I have proof that eternity exists? Do I have proof that there is life after death? No, I don't. But I do know one thing for sure. That I don't suffer when I think of my dad anymore because he is not dead and gone, he is just beyond at the next stop where we all will go when we transition…and that makes me feel happier which is my choice in life.

Let Me Give You A "Peace" of My Heart

Now that we have called the BS (Belief Systems) out in our head/ mind that help and hurt our ability to move from Loss into Faith, it's time to balance and heal our hearts too.

There are two extremes that I often see people get stuck in from loss…on one end they wallow, marinade, and "ruin-ade" in it and end up trapped in unhappiness, or at the other end in an effort to escape the sadness, they bury the pain, which doesn't go away but sits in the dark, eventually growing mold.

Those who grow up being told not to cry or feel sad especially in public, sing the "I'm Okay," song to the tune of Denial, and then throw themselves into activity or a bathtub of gin to try to forget quickly, or lash out in anger for revenge and retaliation. These coping mechanisms work…until they don't. A life coach friend of mine, Wendy Darling, told me about a great book titled "Feelings Buried Alive Never Die." On the other extreme, those who grow up with "I feel therefore I am" can get stuck marinating in the low vibration of grief, which can overwhelm them to the point of paralysis.

So, where's the balance? It's okay and normal and a beautiful part of life to feel sad. The way through pain is to feel it fully and let tears wash away the pain. As I wrote in the OC Register article, 'Tears are the disinfectant that keep the heart soft and out of festering bitterness'. Those words came to me as a direct result of being in the library that day. So, cry. It is so critical to feel the raw pain fully through the first few months of loss. Being held, being hugged, being looked into, being present, being reminded of how precious life is, being okay with being numb, hurt, angry, sad, confused, disoriented, pissed off, in soul-wrenching pain.... all of those feelings are normal. Wendy shared with me a brilliant 'how to comfort ourselves through the pain' analogy. Think of how you would comfort a child who just got hurt from falling or hit...you enfold them into your arms and just let them cry and murmur words of love. "It's okay. You will be okay. It's okay to cry. Yes, it hurts. Go ahead and cry. I've got you." That's what we can do for ourselves. When I am sad, I've picked up the blissipline of hugging myself and allowing my BCS to talk to my sad one with those words exactly. For how long? There's no magic formula, but I do know that when you can sit with the pain of loss and not try to escape ignore or marinade in it, you can get out the other side. And we can start that process in the Into Action section that follows.

Learning in Action with Balance Tools

The following Balance exercises are designed to help heal your mind and your heart and clean out the infection stemming from Loss that keeps us from being Happy.

☯ Balance Tool: Remembering Them Whole

One of the ways we get stuck in the marinade of loss is by only remembering our loved ones in the last day, month or year of their life. If they suffered from a chronic illness, or had an acute attack, we weep remembering the suffering or the dramatic end, and it feeds into the hole of loss. When my dad was dying of lymphoma, after the doctors finally figured out the reason for the bruises and ran battery after battery of tests over a 4-month period, and then finally starting chemotherapy, which was worse than cancer, I had the bright idea to write a book about my dad. I wrote in each chapter a memory of something he had taught me, had done for me, had made a difference in my life about…and it was about 18 chapters long. I then spent the time by his bedside the last few months he was alive, reading him the book. A chapter a day on the days he was able to listen and smile and nod and react. It was the most precious time with him that I will never forget. So, if you are still suffering from a loss that happened a long time ago, and lowering your ability to be happy 88% of the time, use the next Balance tool to record and remember them whole so you can move past the suffering pain of loss into faith.

☯ Balance Tool: Feel it Fully

If you can, drive to the beach or lake or mountains where you can be supported in this exercise by Mother Nature. Bring a photo album of your loved one and a blank book notepad and your favorite pen. Give yourself an afternoon and bring tissues. Pets are great as companions in case you need a hug in between chapters. That's why I call them 'Unconditional Dogs.' Sorry, cat lovers, but I am allergic to them. Let your Balanced Centered Self as described in Chapter 1 guide you in the following exercise.

- Take some time right now, sit and write. Breathe in. Exhale and release all the stories and the drama onto paper.
- Tell me about your loved one, their name, their place in your life, their best 88% qualities and their 12% not so best.
- And now going through the photo album, let the pictures take you back to write every chapter, using the prompt: Thank you _____ for teaching me about _____. Remember the time…
- Write as many chapters you can, and know that you can always add more later.

THIS IS A BOOK ABOUT…

Chapter 1:

_____

_____

_____

_____

_____

_____

_____

Chapter 2:

_____

_____

_____

_____

_____

_____

_____

Chapter 3:

_____

_____

Chapter 4:

Chapter 5:

_____

_____

_____

Chapter 6:

_____

_____

_____

_____

_____

_____

Chapter 7:

_____

_____

_____

_____

_____

_____

_____

Chapter 8:

_____

_____

_____

_____

_____

_____

_____

_____

If your loved one is still alive, you now have something to converse about other than how they are feeling about their illness, or how the doctors and nurses are not doing enough, or how the treatment is going. I know that now when I call my mother, who has Parkinson's, it's an arduous conversation talking about all of her aches and pains, and that it's much more fun when I interject an "remember when, Mom" especially when I add a point of appreciation to the memory.

If your loved one has already transitioned, then on their anniversaries when you usually stay in bed missing them and crying and falling deeper and deeper into a hole of sadness, balance the natural grief with all of the wonderful joyous and happy memories. I also encourage parents to share stories of their parents on passing anniversaries, especially funny ones. I may tear up but there's an equal amount of laughter when I share the funny stories too about my father with my daughters. Another fun twist is to play the genetic game with your kids when remembering the grandparents. This is where did you get this trait from…well you many not remember _____, but your uncle _____ (who now is on the other side) used to _____.

The key is to feel the sadness, but catch yourself before you fall into a wallow. Balance out the sadness and pain of loss by using your Power of Choice to remember the joy again…what wonderful things happened because that individual was a part of your life. In time, you will have more balance in how you remember and celebrate and elevate, instead of falling into the pain pit.

☯ Balance Tool: Soothing the Voices in Our Head

It is also helpful to revisit some of your characters that we got in touch with in the first chapter, who take up space in our heads and hearts. When we are feeling the pain of loss, you may hear the voices in your head saying:

The Critic:

> "Just suck it up…quit crying whining and moaning…so they
>   died, everyone dies"
> "You never told them you loved them before they died"
> "If you had been more attentive they wouldn't have killed
>   themselves"
> "If they had been more careful, this never would have happened"
> "Why do the good guys always die first? You are being punished"
> "Someone is going to pay for this"
> "I will NEVER forgive and forget!"
> "Don't cry, show how strong you are"
> The Sad One:
> "I want to cry, but I am afraid that if I start, I won't ever stop."
> "I really miss them"
> "I really want to die…I can't survive without them"

And so again, strengthening your BCS Balanced Center Self to soothe the voices is the key to moving through the pain pit, finding the bottom, making your way up out of the black hole and back into the Light.

The BCS to the Sad One:

> "Yes, my beautiful, sad one, of course, you miss them. You
> loved them and wanted to be together forever. And sweetheart,
> they really are not extinguished…they have moved to a dif-

ferent place…one that we can't see with our eyes but where we will one day meet up with them again. And, in the meantime, they are still here in our hearts, loving us, supporting us, watching us with love and pride. And they are now with our other friends, family and pets who have also transitioned. It's okay to feel sad, it's okay to cry…tears are the disinfectant that keep your heart soft so just lean your head on my shoulder and let your tears fall. When they subside, and they will, I will take your hand and we'll go do something that will help us remember the good times we had with them. And their love is like the wind now…we can't see them but we can still feel them if we stop, close our eyes and feel."

The BCS to the Critic:

"Darling, I hear you…you're mad, you're looking for a reason for why this happened, you are looking for someone or something to blame so that you can feel better. You want vindication, you want to punish, you want to understand…let's just take a deep breath. Let's not rush into looking for blame. We don't know why…and we may never know why…and I know you're just trying to make sense out of this but lashing out is not going to help our mental, emotional or physical health.

And please don't stifle our little Sad One. It's okay to cry, it's okay to release that pain. It's normal to be sad…and mad, but let's balance it out with some time to also be at peace. Have a seat dear one…you must be tired yelling and criticizing. I got this, you can relax.

I don't know why this happened but I do know that we live in a Friendly Universe…even when it doesn't look like it. I know that a year knows what a day doesn't, that more will be revealed, that everything happens for our Divine and Best Good and in time we may know why. I know that the best question that I can ask us is "When our hearts are broken open

by loss…what is trying to emerge from the gap…what qualities, gifts and abilities are being developed…is it for more love?
more compassion? more understanding? And can I choose to
balance and focus on that end of the loss stick so that I can feel
less pain and more faith in the good? Because ultimately, if I
stay in the suffering feeling of loss, I rob myself of happiness. I
can feel the loss fully and then rise out of the pain and ask what
beautiful plant can sprout from this loss?"

☯ Balance Tool: FTG Find the Good

What if tragedy and loss have a role in our lives? Is it possible that
when natural disasters happen it serves as a catalyst to bring us closer as
a human race erasing borders that keep us one up and one down? What
if tragedy occurs to encourage us to be planet patriots and care for each
other instead of being competing hoarding country nationals? What if
murder, rape, and all manner of horror brings us to a place of healing…to
shine a light on those areas in our lives and in the systems that we operate
in that need attention? What if every tragedy is an opportunity to unite
and care and form positive meaningful collaborative action and relationships? What if alchemy is the order of the day? What if the butterfly whose
death as a caterpillar is the role model for us as human beings? That in
order to truly fly, we do have to break down, experience pain, discomfort,
limitations, and darkness in order to emerge into the Light, both as individuals and as a collective society. If I choose to believe that, then I won't
spend the rest of my life resenting and suffering from tragic loss.

So, let's practice using the Balance tool FTG:

What if, as difficult as it feels, what if this loss was inevitable? What if
it could not be avoided, what if there was nothing different that you or
anyone else could have done to change the outcome? What if you were
supposed to say goodbye? What if that person was supposed to commit
the crime? What if, as horrible as it played out, there was something that
was supposed to emerge from the darkness? What good can come out
of this loss? What skill quality or ability was developed or expanded as

a direct result of the loss? What developed in you as a result of this happening? What can I stop fighting against so that I can expand myself and others? What is possible now in your life? What is possible now in the lives around you? Yes, you may have to dig really, really deep but there are seeds there to find.

> *Frederick*: During the Rwandan Genocide, the army came and one of the commanders chopped off my hands with a blunt machete, because I refused to shoot innocent people. I hated. I never thought I would ever forgive and I certainly could not forget. I have stumps now. I lost many friends and family members. How could a loving God allow this to happen? Well, after the initial grief and anger made its way in and through me, I realized that nothing good would ever happen if I could not allow the losses go. I choose to believe that I have a special role in my life because of the loss. In fact, I opened a rehabilitation center in my hometown that helps many individuals like me who have lost limbs help each other heal so that nothing like this can ever happen again. I know that this Center is the purpose of my life and it is rewarding beyond imagination. I can now say that I am grateful for what happened to me"

Frederick is a shining example of using this Balance tool to its fullest rewarding capacity.

Now it's your turn to create your own FTG List. Take a breath and find the good. Write what you can. Come back to it. Ask the Friendly Universe for answers… change your Why?! to What good can come out of this?

My FTG FIND THE GOOD LIST

- _____

- _____

- _____

- _____
- _____
- _____
- _____
- _____

We started this chapter in the pain and suffering of losing someone we couldn't let go of and the grip was squeezing our ability to feel happy 88% of the time. Feeling fully the pain of Loss leads us into a Faith that restores us to the fullness and beauty of what it means to be alive. Now that you have balanced your mind and your heart back to health, it's time to turn the flashlight onto another kind of loss which gives us another way to happiness… from Heartbreak back into Love.

CHAPTER 3

Out of Heartbreak...into Love

Have you ever had your heart broken? I know many people who have had "that one" relationship where all their hopes and dreams were put like eggs in one basket that ended up dropped and cracked into a million pieces. And the collateral damage is the construction of a huge protective wall that we think will keep out any further heart assaults, but ends up shielding us from the ability to ever purely love again. If you would like to make sure that you are thawed out enough to have true love in your relationships, play along with me in this chapter.

Sit comfortably, gently close your eyes, breathe, and bring back the memory of that heartbreak. Now open your eyes and...

CHECK ALL THAT APPLY:

- ❑ My heart hurts.
- ❑ My heart aches.
- ❑ I'm broken.
- ❑ I will never be whole again.
- ❑ I can't stand up.
- ❑ I never thought I would actually feel like my heart is broken, literally.
- ❑ What did I do to deserve this?
- ❑ How could they do this to me?
- ❑ I have done nothing to warrant such cruel and unusual

punishment.
- ❏ I can't stop crying.
- ❏ He said he would grow old with me.
- ❏ She promised…
- ❏ I never knew she could be so cruel.
- ❏ How could he betray me like that?
- ❏ What did I ever do to deserve to be cut like this?
- ❏ I will never love again.
- ❏ I will never trust again.
- ❏ No one will get close enough to me to hurt me again.
- ❏ I might as well just end it all…I can't go on.
- ❏ Please stop the pain.
- ❏ I will never recover from this.
- ❏ I will never feel alive again.
- ❏ I'm dying inside and I can't…

Sound Familiar?

If you've checked more than half, I know how you feel…

Shay: "How can I bounce back from this? We met in college, I loved her at first sight. I thought we were going to grow old together. I don't understand… I gave her everything she wanted and now she doesn't love me anymore? I feel like there's a knife in my chest that I'll never be able to remove."

Marie: "She found me on Facebook, and told me that my high school sweetheart husband had cheated on me with her less than 6 months after my fairytale wedding. And now she is pregnant with his child. I can't stop crying, and it's been more than a year. I cycle between pure hatred and gut-wrenching sadness. How could he have done this to me?"

Heartbreak is one of the most difficult places to come out of into happiness. Not only has the rug been pulled out from under you, every fundamental belief about the goodness of people is also shaken. Friends feel bad for you for a while, but then the bitterness takes root and gets infected so that it taints every other relationship that you have, with anger, resentment, cynicism, hopelessness, and emptiness. My clients swear that they will never allow themselves to fall in love again. How many people do you know that have been scarred by their first 'heartbreak hotel,' and that every relationship is a threat to returning to that hotel room again?

Let Me Give You A "Peace" of My Mind

In the beginning…

You meet someone and they look at you and you look at them and its magic. The world looks bright, colorful, you have sweet words to savor throughout the day, words spoken, written, texted, emailed, sent in poetry, cards… all igniting the warm feeling of expansion which makes you feel like you can soar. Promises are made with words like 'always' and 'forever,' which are sweet every-things whispered in our ears. Women who love to "futurize" or as I call it "go to MSU University (Make Shit-ake Up)" have the names of their grandchildren chosen, have the house, neighborhood and social calendar planned. Men who really want to believe that they scored such a hottie stand a little taller and keep that voice that says, 'it's too good to be true' at bay.

And then the ceiling caves in from the weight of betrayal. Some cheat, some lie, some beat, some leave without a word, some have the *cajones* to tell you they just don't feel the same way anymore. Or it ends in a tragedy where they die and leave you alone. They all culminate at the same STOP sign. And we fall apart. And vow to never allow anyone to see our hearts open again. EVER. The rest of your life becomes a defensive play, protecting your heart from ever being broken again. Happiness takes a permanent nose dive, because that protective stance will keep you from feeling love from the inside out.

> *Danielle*: I've been dumped, cheated on, mistreated and ignored by one too many men. I will never date again. Loneliness is my best friend. I don't need a man to complete me. F%^$@ men. No one will ever have the chance to hurt me again. I hate being lonely, but I hate leaving myself open for more pain yet again!

I'm not arguing that you didn't get hurt. Yes, having someone that you thought would return that feeling and keep the promise of forever growing old holding hands babysitting the grandkids break the promise feels like a knife. It's a deep wound. You deserve to cry. You deserve to stomp your feet. You deserve to put your face in a pillow and sob and not bathe or change your clothes for a few days, yes. But to lock yourself up for the rest of your life for fear of having your heart broken again? Really? Is life really over from one heartbreak? Are our hearts really that fragile? Should all manner of mates now suffer from your one bad experience? Do you really want to give up on the wonder of love in life after just one strike out? That's a steep price to pay for one betrayal.

I am not minimizing how you are feeling. I have had my heart broken, more than once actually. And I also swore like Sherry, including using the F word. But life is longer than one stay at heartbreak hotel. But it's your choice… remember the Power of Choice. I am encouraging you if you are ready, to take another look and move from Heartbreak back into Love and more Happiness.

Foundation Peace: Choose Your Truth

Here's the BS (Belief Systems) that keep us stuck in Heartbreak:

- There's only one that can be the love of my life, and once that ends, I am forever doomed to be alone.
- I can never trust again.
- Men are out to break my heart.
- Women are out to cheat me.
- True love is supposed to last forever.
- No matter how good it gets, I will get let down.
- I already had the love of my life, I'm fine on my own.
- I will never find anyone like her again.
- I don't feel the same way about anyone else.
- I lost a piece of me and I will never feel whole again.
- I need someone to complete me.
- I will never find anyone to love me as I am.

So, what is the Truth?

The truth is that somewhere down the line we bought into some Belief Systems that keep us in pain after heartbreak. Religion tells us that if we meet someone and make a commitment before God and man, that no matter how horrific things are, you stay together no matter what because you don't get to part until death. No thanks to Cinderella, we believe that we will meet a Prince Charming who knows our shoe size and that they will make us happily ever after. And that if Prince Charming leaves to cheat with your step-sister, well there is no story like that. Our culture is steeped with romance movies, books, photos, news, gossip, myths, commercials that continue to keep us in the BS... thinking that there is only one love so if that doesn't work, life is over. That love is supposed to be easy and that it comes with a lifetime guarantee. That our mates are perfect and don't make mistakes and by default neither do we. So, when there is betrayal or loss of "the one", we get stuck in heartbreak, afraid to love again, afraid to be vulnerable, afraid to date, afraid to touch and be touched literally and figuratively.

The good news is that we can choose a different truth, belief systems that give us an unlimited chance at love for our entire lifetime... so that marriage vows, Cinderella and religion don't have to keep us from one of the most poignant gifts of life—intimate relationships. That's why I coined the term Book of Romance which describes a more hopeful look at relationships because we are capable of having more than one chapter of this life gift. It doesn't have to have a hundred chapters, but it can certainly have more than one. Yes, by continuing to be open to write, we can find our way out of heartbreak back into love.

Steps to Checking out of your Heartbreak Hotel:

Step1: Stop believing and acting like we have to find someone to complete us.

We can blame Jerry McGuire or all of the movies and bedtime stories and fairy tales that insist that there is something missing unless you have a partner. Now before you accuse me of being happily divorced and advocating being single, I am not. But hear me out. What sounds better to you… two half people coming together to make a whole so that if one person leaves, you are only a half a person and then damaged? Or is it possible that as a whole person, you can be wholesome and whole-more and complete and happy with your own company 88% of the time? You enjoy your own company when you are alone, and when you are attracted to someone, choose to be with another whole-some and whole-more and complete romantic partner that you are happy with 88% of the time. Then regardless of if they are present or not, you are 88% happy in your relationship with yourself and with them. Breathe. What a concept! That means that all of the drama and anxiety of "where are they" "what are they doing without me" "are they always going to be there" "will they always love me like they do now" "I can't live without them" goes away. Breathe. Wouldn't that be wonderful?! Is it possible?! Yes!

Wanting someone to complete you is a red flag to any prospective partner… that means you are coming into the relationship needy and always looking for something and someone to fill in the blanks. And if they are looking for you to complete them… run. It sounds romantic at first, but it will chew you up and spit you out when it's over. This is not feminism speaking…this is loving yourself first. Diane has this concept down.

> *Diane*: I love going to movies, and I am no longer ashamed or embarrassed to go alone. It used to bother me seeing all the couples holding hands and smooching, it made me miss my ex and I would get sad. And then I realized that I wasn't really missing him, I was missing the idea of seeing a movie with someone I had the hots for. And now that I understand that every romantic relationship is just another chapter in my Book of Romance, I don't feel like I'm missing anything at all. I know that I am a nice, cute, creative, generous, fun-loving, ambitious, witty woman who loves movies and sailing. And that my love life doesn't have to end just because the man who I had limited my life by calling him 'my one and only' has

left because he fell in love with another woman. Sure, I was mad, and hurt, and never wanted to date again. But who was I punishing? Myself. There are plenty of men out there who love movies and sailing and would find me attractive. And there are men out there like me who I can feel a spark of attraction to if I let myself open up to possibilities for an expanded relationship called romance. In the meantime, I am going to enjoy the heck out of this movie! I am grateful to have the anticipation of what's to come untainted by what was!

Having a partner is incredible when two people feel great about themselves and do not need the other person to make them feel good. Of course, a little compliment, gallantry and romance goes far but it isn't the cake, it's the icing. If we can bake our own cake and really know and like ourselves first, then "finding" someone to validate and complete us goes away. Meeting someone that we connect with in an expanding way is so delicious… so that sharing things we already do and love is like desert at every sitting.

Step 2: Stop acting and believing that there is only one

Who started that, anyway? And don't go all crazy thinking that I am going down the polyamorist route. I absolutely believe in committed relationships, and if you don't, no problem, no argument especially since you can't talk back to me right now - ha! But I am challenging the institution of marriage that has young women fantasizing about walking down the aisle with anyone who asks. An institution that says, "till death do us part" even when people change over time, even when they are miserable most of the time together. How many couples do you know who spend more time wishing their partner was different than they are, trying unsuccessfully to change them through charm, cajoling, reasoning, and then threatening with ultimatums? And again, I am not advocating easy divorces either… I think we've swung the pendulum a little too far so that it's too easy to leave now in reaction to the generation where it was almost impossible to leave. There is a balance between staying too long and not staying long enough. But the point of this step is that even if you meet someone and you think they are "the one" and then they end up hurting you emotionally, verbally, physically, and/or you find out that they two of you have changed so much so that there's not enough glue to keep you together anymore, please do not feel you have to stay because they are "the one". Time changes, people change, feelings change and thinking that you are tied till death with "the one" who doesn't act like 'the one" is just plain harmful to you. You can have more than one who will be an 88% match to your 88% again.

For those of you who have had a "love of your life" and they are now on the other side, a.k.a. died and think there's nothing more, that you are 'one and done' and don't need a partner to be happy because no one can ever measure up… think again. Life is too short to not love yourself, and it is also too short not to keep reading and writing in your Book of Romance. Because those initial butterflies, the comfort, the care, the intimate touch, the connection between partners is something that you cannot get anywhere else… not your children, not your friends, not your family… it's just reserved for romance! So, don't throw away the book baby with the bathwater when 'the one' is over. Just turn the page and start a new chapter.

Step 3: It's not a failure if it doesn't last forever!!

When I am asked to comment on why marriages fall apart, I like to point out that a marriage that actually lasts a lifetime is a major miracle if you consider how difficult it is to:

Number One: Meet someone you are actually attracted to. My running average is every 800 men… I literally count at airports and stop at the 800th one on average who I fantasize joining the mile-high club with. Sorry, I couldn't resist.

Number Two: Stay with someone after the initial googoogaga's wear off (about 6 weeks to 6 months depending on where the glass empty or full line is, or how strong denial runs in the relationship.) I actually share my Pregnancy Model of relationships in the next section.

Number Three: People Change... which is normal over time. What's the likelihood that two people who come together actually change in the SAME direction, at the SAME rate, and towards the SAME destination as each other? Pretty unusual, right? Then why do we expect people to stay together forever?!

Using these three rules of engagement, I am surprised we even have as many long-term relationships as we do. Maybe the Pope knew these 3 truths and so marriage was a rule to keep nature from running (away) from its natural course.

> *Trevor*: I hate telling people who I'm dating because when it doesn't work out I get the "oh I'm sorry, what's wrong with her, what's wrong with you" look and questions. The truth is there is nothing wrong with her and nothing wrong with me... it just wasn't a match. And we couldn't have figured it out any other way then spending the time we did together.

Can you imagine what life would be like if everyone started thinking and acting like Trevor? I wish we could all stop seeing relationships as either a forever success or break-up failure. It's not either. We're here on the planet to have great relationships. And when one or both of us are more miserable than happy, it means that it's time to start a new chapter. And there was nothing wrong with the last chapter. No one was the bad guy, no one is to blame and both parties grew learned expanded and loved themselves and each other to a higher level so there's nothing to be sorry for, angry or ashamed of.

Can you buck your BS about relationships only being successful when they last forever? Can you allow yourself to have multiple chapters in your Book of Romance? Can you feel 88% happy with yourself regardless if you are with someone or not, and that you don't need someone to complete you? Can you be happy with your partner 88% of the time? Have I done enough of a sales job for you to check out of Heartbreak Hotel and start a new chapter in your Book of Romance? Yes? Wonderful! Then let's move through the healing process. Let's dig out the root of your heartbreak and apply some Balance Tools to turn the shiitake into fertilizer!

Learning in Action with Balance Tools

☯ Balance Tool: Letting Go of Past Pain... What are the Facts?

Let's go back into the pain of past heartbreak one last time... open the scab and disinfect so you can heal and open yourself up again to Happiness, Joy and Love.

Answer the following questions with the facts:

How did you meet?

_____

_____

_____

_____

What did you love about them?

_____

_____

_____

_____

What did they say to you?

_____

_____

_____

_____

What promises were made?

_____

_____

_____

_____

What happened?

_____

_____

_____

_____

What was the worst part of the whole thing?

_____

_____

_____

_____

If tears are coming now that is good. Remember, tears are the disinfectant that keep your heart soft. Breathe. Stay with the pain, the ache, the feeling of sadness, of loss, of betrayal, of anger, of regret. Write it all down.

Pay attention to what your Critic and Sad One are saying and use the space to get in touch with those voices in your head that are keeping you from checking out of the Heartbreak Hotel.

Critic:

> "How could you have been so stupid to have believed their lies?"
> "You weren't lovable enough or they wouldn't have left, or changed the way they felt."
> "If you hadn't let yourself gain all that weight they would not have been turned off and left."
> "If you had been more attentive or beautiful or smart or successful, they would have stayed."
> "Your parents were right, you are damaged goods."
> "You are destined to be alone."

Add in anything else your Critic is saying to you…

_____

_____

_____

Sad One:

> "I am broken."
> "I am fading away."
> "I am unworthy of love."
> "I am not enough."
> "I am destined to be left."
> "They took their love and left me to fade away"

Add in anything else your Critic is saying to you…

_____

_____

_____

Balanced Centered Self:

> "Thank you, Critic and Sad One, but all of your statements are lies." It's time to work on Loving ourselves."

☯ Balance Tool: Loving Yourself

If we want to check out of Heartbreak Hotel, we have to be able to respond to the lies that keep us stuck in the ranting of the Critic and the Sad One. So, to all the statements you just put to paper, you now have the opportunity to engage in the process of Loving Yourself from the inside out, by strengthening the voice of your Balanced Centered Self. Practice saying:

> "Thank you, critic, I know you're trying to protect me by hating and blaming and shaming…but it's not good for us. That heartbreak was just the end of one relationship. It wasn't

the one and only with no more to come. It was a great relationship especially at the beginning but by the end, it was more pain than gain. I choose to believe that it was a great chapter in our Book of Romance. All of the beautiful things that were said at the beginning of the relationship were true. No one was lying. Everyone said what was in their heart, and it's not helpful to just throw out all relationships and partners just because this one didn't end the way we wanted to. It was real. It was beautiful and it's our job to focus on what was good, so that we can carry over what was great into our next relationship."

Here's what I learned about me, what I liked and didn't like from my last relationship:

- I loved the way he was a gentleman.
- I loved the feeling of being told I was beautiful.
- I loved laughing together.
- I loved the way it felt when we went biking together.
- I loved playing cards together.
- I didn't like the moodiness so next one please, a little less drama.
- I didn't like the broken record stories of his past, so please next one, a little less emotional baggage...maybe just carry-on size ha!
- I didn't like the occasional cruel sarcastic comments about others...next one please kinder.

Now it's your turn.

What I liked and what I would like improved for my next chapter in my Book of Romance.

_____

_____

_____

_____

_____

_____

_____

_____

Every relationship you have, short or long, helps you write a new chapter in your book of romance by giving you a lot of information about what you like and don't like. Because I choose to believe in a Friendly Universe, I believe that it's always 'this or better' so the next chapter will be an improvement on the last one. And, it's my birthright as a precious child of a Friendly Universe to have my desires for an 88% perfect partner met. And there's nothing wrong with ending a relationship where there is not an equal exchange of feeling. Why would you want to stay in a relationship or continue to give it the pedestal trophy title of "the one" when the connection has changed?

There is no need to go back and confront the promise breaker. No need to stand up and rail against the person who broke your heart. Because your heart is not broken. No one can really break your heart. It is a super eternal beautiful, strong, wonderful, caring, loving heart that has more than nine lives. It can get bruised, it can even bleed, but it is never irrevocably broken. If you aren't able to believe that yet, it's okay. Do you believe that I believe it? Then believe that until you can yourself…and you will, I promise.

Foundation Peace: Time to Love Again

So now we're ready for romance again! Romantic relationships are incredible… there's no feeling like it. As I mentioned earlier, but is worth repeating… you can't get that unique loving feeling from your parents, your friends, your children or your co-workers… well maybe in an office romance, but that's another topic and not what I am trying to get at! The intimacy that comes when you let your heart break wide open for romance is special, and it's one of the greatest gifts of life. You are worthy of this kind of love, and you can write long and short chapters in your Book of Romance. Heartbreak is not a lifetime sentence. Yes, relationships are hard. But they don't have to be that hard. It takes work to remain open and not give in to cynicism, or a monastery for that matter. But we are social animals, and I do know now beyond a shadow of a doubt that I am supposed to have romantic relationships… my God did not make me this affectionate, playful, fun-loving, social, attractive (and modest) to be alone enjoying a fireplace or not enjoying the feeling of holding hands. So, I am open to a romantic relationship with an equal partner. My silly, wonderful girlfriend Ann Marie made me start affirming that every day. Still no relationship, but I am getting oodles of attention. These next set of Balance tools are to help ensure your relationships have a great running start into the next chapter in your Book of Romance!

☯ Balance Tool: Priming the Dating Pump

I used to say that dating was like the Wide World of Sports opener; "the thrill of victory and the agony of defeat". See if you relate to any of these statements…

Check all that apply:

- ❏ UGH I HATE DATING
- ❏ All the good ones are gone
- ❏ People lie on their profiles
- ❏ I've had the love of my life and I'm good
- ❏ I can't imagine meeting anyone at my age that would rock my boat…
- ❏ I love myself enough that I really don't need anyone else really….
- ❏ I have had the worst experiences dating…is there a shortcut?

If you're not excited about dating based on your experiences I only have one question. Was it before or after getting to Loving Yourself? Because as a student of the Law of Attraction, I know that all of my dating and relationship trials were not representative of what it could be now because as a needy wanting to be completed half, I attracted another person who was just like me, and/or one who repelled someone like me… the more I wanted commitment, the more he wanted freedom. So, don't give up but make sure you are loving yourself 88% of the time before you try dating.

Another way to prime your dating pump is to stop believing the BS listed above, like "all the good ones are gone'" and "there's no one good enough out there for me". If you don't, then you will definitely see what you believe. There's actually a psychological phenomenon called "The Pygmalion Effect" which takes the old adage "I'll believe it when I see it" and flips it around to "I'll see it when I believe it." The experiments show that people will see scenarios that agree with their Belief Systems before they see data that disproves their BS. What you believe about the dating pool will come true for you. Even if you don't initially believe it, try to start making statements like:

- There are plenty of fish in the sea.
- Now with the internet I can meet hundreds of more candidates for my next chapter in my Romance book.
- I learn something from every relationship whether it lasts a year or a lifetime.
- I am excited to turn the page to see what's next in my book of Romance.

Do you have any other statements that keep you in the highest possible dating vibration? Write them down here:

_____

_____

_____

_____

🌀 Balance Tool: Fix Your Picker

Many of us find ourselves in difficult romantic relationships because we think we can change people. You say you know what you want and then you find someone who doesn't have the characteristics on your list, get together with them anyways and then wonder why there's not a match! I love the way Don Miguel Ruiz, past guest and author of mega-bestseller *The Four Agreements*, describes dating process in his fabulous book, *Mastery of Love*, with "If you want a dog, don't buy a cat!" So, if you know that you abhor smoke, you're a foodie, you love to race sailboats, you enjoy trying new things, you have a strong belief in God, you physically can't have children, and you love snuggling… then DON'T start dating a smoking, agoraphobic, vegetarian, celibate atheist who wants to start a family! And if you know that you are a neat freak, don't pretend that you are easygoing… display yourself as you are, not who you think someone wants you to be. You shop and display yourself in the same marketplace, so show off who you really are… the same way you'd like to know that you are.

Now does that preclude wanting to make yourself the best that you can be? Absolutely not. We'll tackle this opportunity in Chapter 6: On Freedom. But there is a healthy balance between choosing potential and choosing people for who they are and then being resentful when they are not who you want them to be. Let me illustrate with another concept from the *Mastery of Love* by Don Miguel Ruiz.

> If you spend most of your time with someone wishing they were different than they actually are…
> "If he loved me he would pick up after himself" (his place was not neat the first time you had an unplanned visit)
> "If he loved me he would call when he is going to be late" (he's wasn't a clock watcher when you first met)
> "If he loved me he would stop smoking" (he smoked when you first met)
> "If he loved me he would be more affectionate to me in public" (he put that pda—public displays of affection -- were a turnoff on his profile)

…then LET HIM GO so he can find someone who likes him as he is, unchanged for the most part. As much as you hate him the way he is most of the time, I would bet 88 dollars that he isn't crazy about being with someone who constantly wants to change him all the time either.

So, the point of this tool is to know yourself and to know what matches up with that… most of the time. Another one of my relationship coach best friends, Mary Richardson, says that if you get along 80% of the time, that's the best it will be and be happy with that… there's no such thing as perfect! That's a bit tough for yours truly the recovering perfectionist but it is an expectation that will help me be more realistic and less hard on my mate. However, I have upped the percentage to 88% in case you didn't notice! Ha! Next Balance tool can help you answer the question, "When to hold and when to fold?".

☯ Balance Tool: My Pregnancy Model of Relationships

I have a Balanced Trimester theory about relationships. In the first three months, it is a beautiful baby… there's excitement, there's mystery, there's a glow, there's anticipation, expectation, exhilaration, wonder, bliss, warmth, coziness and life is amazing. You make promises to each other based on the glow.

The second trimester things start to pop out and get uncomfortable. The reality of impeding serious change surfaces. Emotions are not all above sea level, irrational mood swings, cravings, upset stomach heart and mind and the reality of who the two people really are in the partnership surfaces. The glow gives way to occasional gas and hot rashes as the imperfect side of each partner erupts. "Forever" words and actions made in the first trimester go underground in the second trimester. The "what happened to opening doors/flowers/sweet somethings/generosity/romance?" song gets played a lot.

In the third trimester, the "Should I stay or should I go" song is played and the couple gets to see if there is enough glue, or the 88% good enough to continue. Between the second and third semesters, it is normal to have relationships end.

The pregnancy of relationships is an important dance to go through. You get a balanced look at each other to see if there's enough crazy glue to keep you together for a longer haul, enough chemistry and common goals to ensure that most of the time you're both 88% happy. If you find out in the second trimester that "reality" has more of a downside than the upside of the "honeymoon", then isn't it better to find out before spending 25 thousand dollars on a wedding? If we can all buy into the Pregnancy dance of testing out partners, then there would be no need to blame ex-partners of not being good enough, or pointing out how they fell short, or how they showed their true colors and were putting up a good front, or lying about who they were. Of course, people want to show their best side in the beginning. And we mean the loving words we say and feel at the beginning when there is strong attraction. There is not an intention to mislead or deceive, it is just the way we want to put our best foot forward. We're not trying to trip up people, at least maybe not until the second trimester! I'm having an Alice in Wonderland moment right now thinking of six impossible things before breakfast, a world where people would go easy on each other in the romance arena. I'm seeing romance as a beautiful dance with infinite possibilities of part-ners and no heartbreak in sight because it's just not a match when the song is over.

☯ Balance Tool: Asking for What You Want

And just for giggles, I am going to end this chapter with a risk-free trial offer. A wise elder once told me to write down 21 things that I would like to have in a partner so I can hold a space open for him to arrive in. So here goes, and you can use the space below to write your own list. If you are with someone, try to write the list as if you aren't with them just to create some affirmative gratitude (or discomfort) in your relationship.

- Love listening to him talk (accent or word vocabulary)
- Love to laugh with him (matching sense of humor)
- Enjoy dining/eating with him (is a foodie)
- Enjoy nature with him (loves finding beauty in me and others)
- Enjoys sailing (been sailboat racing for 19 years)
- Enjoy cuddling with him (affectionate and playful)
- Respect his work/ethic (takes joy and pride in hard work and accomplishment)

- Proud of his character – integrity, honesty, generosity (a good fine specimen of man)
- Proud of his accomplishments (worthy from worthwhile actions, and esteem from esteemable acts)
- Playful with me in quips (clever and witty)
- Plays with me – games, puzzles (competitive but will let me win)
- Travels with me (loves to explore)
- Shares a love of God with me (is a spiritual giant)
- Shares a love of my children with me (secure role model)
- Is attractive to me – eyes, body, height, jaw (chemistry)
- Respects me
- Is Proud of me
- Supports me emotionally and financially (when needed)
- Spoils me
- Is Patient with me
- Makes my toes curl

Now it's your turn… "What I Want in my next Partner to help me write my next chapter in my book of Romance."

My Partner

- _____
- _____
- _____
- _____
- _____
- _____
- _____
- _____
- _____

- _____

- _____

- _____

- _____

- _____

- _____

- _____

- _____

- _____

- _____

- _____

And in the meantime, I am not alone and you are not alone. I have occasional human feelings of loneliness that are not life-threatening as we addressed in Chapter One. I know my Friendly Universe has a playmate for me who is baking in the oven. If I keep opening the oven door, he will come out half-baked. So, when I am not seeing a man to play with, it's because it's not the right time, but NOT because I am not lovable enough. I have an abundance of love from friends and family. And an unchanging limitless abundant and peaceful love from a Universe that loves me and wants my Highest Good. Always. And so do you. However, if you are still stuck and suffering from a heartbreak that has hardened into unforgiveness, the next chapter is just for you. Read on for another way into happiness… out of Hatred into Forgiveness.

CHAPTER 4

Out of Hatred into Forgiveness

- How dare you do that to me.
- How could you do that to me?
- Mothers are supposed to love their daughters.
- Mothers are supposed to think their daughters are beautiful.
- Fathers are supposed to be role models for their sons.
- How could you hurt me like that??
- How sick are you?
- I hate you.
- You are supposed to be a representative of God.
- I trusted you.
- I was an innocent child.
- How could you be so cruel?
- What gives you the right to hurt children like that?
- May you die a horrible death.
- You are a monster.
- How did I get so unlucky to be born into a family so cruel?
- I am so damaged I will never recover.
- I can't trust anyone because of you.
- I hate because of you.
- I want to rip out my hair.
- I want to rip out my heart.
- I can't get the images out of my head.

- My heart is black.
- My heart hurts.
- I will never forgive you.
- You should burn in hell for what you did.
- I can't believe you did that to me.
- Why would you do that to me?
- Why would you say that to me?
- What have I done to you as a child to warrant your violence, your violation, your hatred.

Sound Familiar?

I have heard true accounts of the most horrific things being done to young innocent children by those who are supposed to protect them.

Chris was six when her father started coming into her bedroom to 'say goodnight.' Now, at 56, she can't bear to have a man touch her, and at the same time she is attracted to older men who treat her like crap. She oscillates from red-hot hatred to "I'm FINE as long as I don't ever have to see him again". After 15 years of therapy, she was no closer to peace of mind or peace of heart. Now she is resigned to a meaningless, apathetic life. She refuses to talk about it anymore, from the pain and the shame and the resentment. He is now on his deathbed and her internal terror is tearing her apart.

Take a deep breath. The checklist and example may have stirred up some dark sludge from past pain… I know it did for me just writing it down. This is not an easy chapter. But if you stay with me, know that I am holding your hand on one side, and with my other hand I'm holding a flashlight of Love and Light… to help us go on a cleansing expedition. We are going into that dark hole to find the bottom. Because you are worthy. Because it's time to release the hatred that is eating you up. We're going to dig out all of the shiitake, and then when we are clean, use it as fertilizer to grow the beautiful precious beings that we all are, no matter what happened to us as children. Because it's time, and I know your pain.

Let Me Give You A "Peace" of My Heart

I hated my mom. When I close my eyes, I can still see, feel, and smell the cold marble floor on which I had to stand still on while suffering hours of slaps and screams. I can feel the cold dark fear that I rocked to in my bedroom after the beatings were over. I can feel frightened all over again watching myself run through the house and out the garage trying to escape her hand, her shoe, her stick, her bright red anger that surrounded me for fifteen years. I hated her with an intensity that I buried deep down inside.

I would not be able to cry while being hit because she said that that meant I was not sorry, so I just bowed my head in silence as the ranting would continue on for an average of two hours. I realize now that one of my coping devices was to close my ears inside...and now I have to really focus to listen to people because I've developed a default of leaving space between words that are sent and words that are received.

I always knew when she was nearing the end of the angry deluge because she would call my father over with "Dad, come over here and tell your daughter how bad she is." He would comply and then I would be dismissed to go up the stairs to my room where I would sit and just rock back and forth with the song "Let me die, let me die, let me die..." After a bit, my father would come up the back stairs and come to my side, put his arm around me and try to comfort me for a minute with "It's okay," and then end that comfort zone with "Now go downstairs and tell your mother you're sorry." You see, after I was dismissed, my mom would go from red hot anger to the wailing wall. At the top of her lungs she would bang around the house crying out loud "Poor me, I am so mistreated and disrespected... what did I do to deserve such a bad daughter" over and over again. Her siren of victimhood was so loud and so unsettling to my dad that he had to do something to make her stop. So, at the end of every request he made of me to go and apologize to my mother was rewarded with "Go say 'sorry' and here's a 20$ bill, here's a bike, here's a car, here's a condo..." And so I would do so again and again and again... each time swearing that I would never apologize again, and every time breaking my promise to myself for the goodies, and to make my dad happy. It was a horrible system of checks and balances.

I found out on my 18th birthday, because he thought I was old enough to know, that my mom was actually sent away for a while because the beatings were so bad. I only remember one broken arm but I do remember that in every single picture of the old photo album, showed a very unhappy and solemn little Chinese girl.

In school, I pretended that everything was okay. I held a common BS Belief System that says, "The past is past. You can't go back and change it so don't bother looking at it at all. Bury your head in the sand and don't address it. Keep it out of sight, out of mind, don't care, don't let it show, you're not being impacted at all by the horrible details of the crime." This approach resembles the garbage disposal truck that I described earlier, that what you press down and repress down will turn into noxious gas at some point, usually at the midlife point, and leak into all of your life interactions. In other words, what you don't deal with will come back and deal with you!! If you do not address and assess and work through past pain, it will come back around and bite you in the butt. So, burying your head in the sand doesn't work except to keep you from happiness 88% of the time.

On the other hand, some people will constantly be triggered by people places and things that remind them of the horror of their past pain so they cannot get to a place of peace with the past. They may go to therapy for 15 years, and every other session ends with them crying in anger about their past painful experiences with no relief in sight. Yes there is a balanced solution.

On the outside, I actually looked like I was okay. I threw myself into achievement, trying to get love from outside approval. Every 'Wow, you're amazing' would give me a minute of relief but then I would hear my Critic say, "You're not that good, you're fat ugly and clumsy just like your mother says you are… they don't really know you and if they did, they wouldn't like you anymore." This path of overachievement to mask abuse is a road often travelled. Many abused children become very successful in life, burying the memories, the pain, and the past. We try to trick ourselves and are quick to answer, "I'm FINE!!" which actually stands for Fed-up (wink), Irrational, Neurotic, and Emotional! But when I came off stage, everything was not okay. When there was downtime, usually enhanced by a single malt scotch, I would inevitably start crying about how unfair life was, how hurt I was, how violated I was by my mother, and how I would never be able to catch up with others who had a normal loving childhood.

I have since found out that normal loving childhoods are an extremely rare. In fact, surprise surprise, I became a psychology major in college and now know that that I am not the minority when it comes to a horrific childhood. As I mentioned in the Preface, *Psychology Today* says that 70% of children grow up in dysfunctional homes. Oprah says that it's more like 8 out of 10 kids who come from unsafe homes. I just heard at a conference that it's up as high as 93% that are raised in harm's way with abuse of some kind… verbal, physical, sexual, neglect, abandonment, or more. That means that the majority of us are walking wounded. It is not surprising to me that as many as one in four Americans are now on anti-depressants and anti-anxiety medication with those statistics. The majority of my clients follow my pattern of coping… hard-working driven perfectionism that threatens to drive them off of a cliff in mid-life. The workaholic that works…until it stops working.

Besides not listening, my other coping devices included work hard play harder, perfectionism, a workaholic ethic, fight and flight, justified anger, and rage. With Psychology as my major I was consciously and unconsciously trying to help myself heal through helping others. But that seething cesspool of anger and resentment led me to darker and darker places in my head which resulted in a difficulty forming healthy relationships with myself and others.

My unresolved but underground anger and pain attracted me to a man who helped me feel as unlovable as I did growing up. Like many children of abuse, I chose a man to marry who was just as emotionally unavailable as my mom was, and I tried to fix that. If I could make him love me, then maybe my mom finally would too. He did not physically abuse me, but the cruel silence and frustrating inability to make him love me was a very familiar feeling. I felt the same way I did growing up in my 9.2 years of marriage, always going to the tractor for milk… trying to find love where there was none to be found.

If my hatred of my mother wasn't enough of a bitter pill to swallow, I also picked a man who would cost me millions of dollars in a lost company I had built and in a settlement that the judge told me was fair because "you wanted equal rights!" Yes, I had an ugly divorce which just added to the hatred already seething below my surface. There was glue on my car and humiliation in my hometown as he posted ads all over my small hometown that said, "Asian woman disillusioned with marriage seeking Asian or Caucasian woman." He had found this ad on Craig's List, photocopied and distributed it so that soon there was a rumor spreading around town amongst the preschool moms that my website had naked women on it. He also would tell people I was obese so that when they met me after the divorce, they would say, "You're not obese!" Interesting how my mom's message that I was fat and ugly carried on to my marriage. Hardest to take was the hundreds, maybe thousands of rejections which kept me starving for intimacy. And so, in the two decades after I left my home, I was super successful on the outside and super broken on the inside. I hated my mother for what she did to me as a child, and I hated my "wasband," another one of my trying to be funny terms for ex-husband, for what he did to me as an adult.

If you're wondering why I am airing out all of my dirty laundry here, it is for one reason only. Anyone who says, "you just don't understand," I can say "yes, I do understand." Maybe our details are different, but the feeling of extreme hatred I absolutely know. And I also know that much of what has happened puts me in a position of justified anger. However, justified anger is a double-edged sword. Yes, I deserve to be spitting angry at both my mom and my 'wasband.' Even if you heard their side of the story, I would still wager that I got the shaft end of the deal. But eventually being so hatefully angry was killing me. I was exhausted holding on to justified resentment. No matter what good happened in my life, I would always return to bitterness. Every telling of the true story would keep me boiling and marinating in anger and hostility. My hatred was robbing me of happiness every single day. Is your hatred blocking your ability to fully love yourself and others? Are you happy? Are you ready to jump out of your own pot of hatred? Yes? Don't worry, I'm here to help catch you.

Let Me Give You A "Peace" of My Mind

I tried a number of ways to jump out of my boiling pot of hatred. First. I tried moving away from home, as far away as I could from my mother… a geographical fix. Like many abused kids, we physically distance ourselves from the violator and pretend that we are just F.I.N.E.! We keep grandchildren away from them because we are afraid of what they might do to our children and are justified in the action because of the past. "They" deserve to be punished over and over again. We try to even up the score from their past ugly treatment of us. The distance does give some relief for a little while but violators can continue to live in your head so the expression "out of sight out of mind" isn't always accurate. I still nursed my justified anger towards her across the miles. I actually did not talk to my mom for eight years, when she was furious with me for not signing away my rights to my father's estate after he passed from lymphoma. The silent treatment didn't make things better either.

I tried numbing the pain through drugs and alcohol which worked while the altered state was altered, but waking up hungover and losing hours and days began to outweigh the hours of relief I was getting. And to add insult to injury, while I was drunk I would wail and cry with so much self-pity I began to lose my party buddies who were tired of the "who done me wrong" song. This song played in the background for every relationship, and so every relationship failed. Bitterness grew deep roots so year after year, the resentment shuffled into more and more space on the inside. Soon the F#$@% You song spread from the original violator to innocent victims whose verdict had not yet come in.

Sheila: I remember the pain of the broken promises, the betrayal, the abandonment. All men became victims... I could hurt them the same way he hurt me. The pain in their eyes was like a drug... I was getting revenge. But the drug wore off and I would feel the sickening shame of being so cruel.

Revenge and retaliation were like drugs, an initial high and then serious consequences afterwards. Trying to release hatred with more hatred is like pouring gas on a fire. Thich Nhat Hanh has a great proverb:

"If your house is on fire, the most urgent thing to do is to go back and try to put out the fire, not to run after the person you believe to be the arsonist. If you run after the person you suspect has burned your house, your house will burn down while you are chasing him or her. That is not wise. You must go back and put out the fire. So when you are angry, if you continue to interact with or argue with the other person, if you try to punish her, you are acting exactly like someone who runs after the arsonist while everything goes up in flames."

— Thich Nhat Hanh

Your teeth might be clenched right now saying, "I will never forgive him. It's not right. It's too much to ask. I hate him." It's true: hatred that stems from justifiable anger is one of the most difficult emotions to "get over" to the other side. What brought me relief from the guillotine of justified anger was an understanding not of the horrible act but by an understanding of what my red-hot song of anguish was doing to myself and my relationships. My unwillingness to forgive was killing me from the inside out.

One of the reasons I was unwilling to forgive was because "I can't forgive because that means I am condoning that horrific behavior!" How can you forgive someone who hurts children? How can you forgive someone who shoots his ex-girlfriend and then shoots innocent people around her? How can you forgive someone who tortures people? How can you forgive someone who sends people to death camps? How do you forgive someone who is supposed to protect you and inflicts harm on you instead?"

Forgiveness, like happiness is a choice. It does not mean that you condone but it does mean you choose to stop railing against it. You stop putting yourself in harm's way. You love yourself enough to let go of the rope that keeps you tied up in knots. Because those knots will eventually become tourniquets that cut off your own circulation, not theirs.

Forgiveness is the most effective way out of hatred. I know I know, you say "OH! I forgive but I will NEVER FORGET!! Then you might as well not forgive. Because every time you remember, your memory will trigger another handgun of anger which will turn you back into a burning ember… one more time. Trust me, I tried that route. Now, I am not advocating amnesia. Of course, you will remember. But choosing NOT TO FORGET does keep the memory alive like a sharp knife ready to stab anyone who remotely resembles your past pain. It is like a Bandaid approach that covers the wound but as soon as it gets wet or dirty, the scab gets picked off and we bleed all over again. So what do I mean by out of Hatred into Forgiveness?

Foundational Peace: Out of Hatred into Forgiveness

Forgiveness is not understanding. I will never understand why some people do the horrible things they do. I can try to understand, I can probably trace their crime to one done to them. I can make up a story that might help me have empathy with them. I may even find the magic explanation that leads me to say "Oh, I guess I could see how that justified their horrific actions". But understanding is not the key to forgiveness. We can get tangled up in the search for meaning when it comes to violation.

Forgiveness is simply a gift to yourself. A gift of relief. A gift of good health. A gift of healthy relationships. Because when you refuse to forgive, you can't isolate your angry bitter resentful ugly feelings to just the perpetrator. It starts to creep into the crevices of your heart, mind and soul…and now the medical community is confirming that it also creeps into your body as well. Dr. Deepak Chopra suggests that there are two emotions that harm the cellular functioning in our body… anger and hostility, which are cousins to the hatred we're addressing here. So refusing to forgive, staying trapped in the intensity of hatred either above or below the surface will hurt you. Haven't you been hurt enough? Are you ready to move out of Hatred? Then let's learn some Balance Tools to soothe ourselves out of hatred into happiness.

Learning in Action with Balance Tools

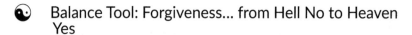 ### Balance Tool: Forgiveness… from Hell No to Heaven Yes

Hatred hurts you more than it hurts the violator. I love the saying "Resentment (another cousin of Hatred) is like drinking poison thinking the other person will die." My Marissa-ism version of that is "I HATE looking at you so I'm going to gouge out my own eye!" Hatred hurts your relationships, hurts your immune system, hurts your well-being, hurts your good nature, kills your ability to have light-hearted fun, kills laughter, kills joy, kills opportunity… need I continue?

So how do I stop hating my mother? How do you stop hating your violator? How do we move into the Light? We start by digging out the root of hatred with the shovel of Forgiveness.

I'll never forget the moment that my forgiveness for my mother was birthed. At an Agape International Spiritual Center class titled "Universal Principles of Spirituality", Dr. Michael Bernard Beckwith, Founder and Director, also affectionately now known as "my big brother" gave me a life-turning concept that started my forgiveness ball rolling. He was actually working with another woman who said, "I can forgive my ex-husband, as hard as that is, but I absolutely cannot forgive my mother for what she did to me as a child". My ears perked up and I sat up straight in my chair! Here's the magic that I'd like you to see if you can get in the middle of with your hatred. Wherever I have written "mom", you put in the name of your violator.

Take a deep breath.

Now think back to the relationship with your mom. What if nothing changed and it was supposed to be exactly as it was... and from that entire experience your heart was broken, yes, but broken wide open. If nothing changed and your mom was supposed to do and be exactly as she was, was there any quality gift or ability that was birthed in you as a direct result of who she was to you??

Breathe and sit with this scenario. Try to ignore your internal Critic's voice that says, "But it's not supposed to happen like that".

Again, what if nothing changed... was there any part of me that grew stronger as a direct result of my mom being exactly the way she was?

Well yes, I grew my ability to be:

- independent,
- self-sufficient,
- strong,
- self-reliant,
- more compassionate,
- more understanding,
- more resilient...

Now you fill in the blanks here: It grew my ability to be...

_____

_____

_____

_____

_____

_____

_____

Okay, do you like those part of yourself?

Well, actually yes, I do! Do you?

If your internal Critic is saying "but couldn't you have developed those qualities without being beaten?" Your Balanced Centered Self can say "Yes maybe, maybe not, but most definitely I did from my mom being exactly as she was!"

Breathe.

So maybe someday you can even thank your mom for helping you develop those qualities… whoa now, Dr. Beckwith, let's not carry that too far! But seriously, I actually have been able to do just that… slowly, bit by bit, after building strength in my BCS to choose this frame with which to see my mom.

The main shift is that you stop seeing yourself as a helpless hurt victim… and instead, see the pain as alchemy. My favorite story to illustrate this concept are the 2 Rocks who had a home in a museum store in New Mexico. Everyday people would come into the store and remark about how beautiful the one Rock was. The Sculpted Rock had incredible lines and planes and the light would glisten around its shape. The other Rock was an un-chiseled chunk and just sat in a corner with very little attention. Day after day the Corner Rock would listen to people 'ooh and ah' over the Sculptured Rock and finally after years of this, the Corner Rock finally calls out. "I AM SICK AND TIRED OF LISTENING TO THE PRAISE FOR THE SCULPTED ROCK!!! IT'S NOT FAIR!! NO ONE EVER SAYS I AM BEAUTIFUL!! MAKE PEOPLE STOP IT, IT'S NOT VERY NICE OR FAIR FOR ME!!!" Life gently turns to the Corner Rock and says, "My Child, you are my beloved, but every time I come near you to help shape and chisel you, you cry out 'NO, NO, NO, THAT HURTS… STOP… NO MORE PAIN' and so I leave you be."

Moral of the story? Life shapes us with chiseling, and sometimes it is painful, but pain is necessary to grow in life. The caterpillar is not comfortable losing its shape, and sitting in a stifling sac growing its wings. The chick is almost suffocated by its own poisonous gas from its poop inside the shell before it pecks its way out into life. If you can shift the way you see what happened to us as abused children as a part of our birthing and growing process and NOT as undue punishment that leads us to justified anger, then we can stop reliving the Pain from our Past igniting Hatred over and over again. To stop lamenting, "WHY ME?" and ask instead "What was birthed in me?" is a Powerful Balance tool that launches us into Happiness 88% of the time. Because Pain is mandatory but suffering is optional!

Balance Tool: Forgiving Mothers

For those who have mother hatred issues, there are a few bonus Balance Tools that have helped myself and my clients put their forgiveness practice on steroids because "If it's not one thing, it's your mother!" And there are only two times in your life when you don't have mother issues… when you're born and when you die! One of my past guests, Edwene Gaines, has a lovely saying about mothers: "Your mother's only job was to pop you out…the rest is gravy!" What would happen if you released all of your expectations of what a "normal loving mother" should be say or do? Then any bit of positive contribution could be recognized as gravy… which is much more pleasant than a litany of deficits.

Another frame that helps me keep my forgiveness intact for my mom is to constantly remind myself that she really truly believed that she was being a loving mother in everything she was doing. This is a frame that takes a firm choice to see. In my case I was lucky, I actually got an unbelievable apology from my mom. She explained the circumstances in her life, her own mother's desired abortion since she was pregnant at the unbelievable age of 48 with my mom, an unrequited love, a mismatched marriage with my dad… it did help me better understand the place of deficit that she came from. Her lashing out in frustrated anger at me made more sense. I still don't condone her behavior, but by seeing her motivation behind her abuse… her helpless reaction to her own triggers helped me find some compassion for her own pain and certainly helped me say in all earnestness "She did the very best that she could…if she could have done better, she would have". My mom truly wanted me to be thin and happy and believed that by telling me "the truth," that I was fat ugly and clumsy, was going to motivate me to be better. I still don't like that she thinks a mother's love gives her *carte blanche* to say mean things, but I can let it go much easier now without it becoming a burning, angry, hate-filled house fire again. Because, again, it is not about understanding why… it is about loving myself enough to choose not to be in hatred any more.

☯ Balance Tool: My Big Brother's Forgiveness Exercise

In addition to the reframe I learned in class from Michael Bernard Beckwith, I also learned a powerful forgiveness exercise from his book that helps remove the edges of unforgiveness. You can find this exercise in his beautiful book "Spiritual Liberation" on page 17.

Find a quiet place to meditate.

Take a breath…and release all the stories and the drama.

Now gently picture the person you want to release your hatred of sitting in front of you. Not too close, but close enough to be able to see their eyes in your mind's eye.

Now repeat the following:

> "I forgive you and set you free. Your actions no longer have power over me. I acknowledge that you are doing the best that you can, and I honor you in your process of unfoldment. You are free and I am free. All is well between us. Peace is the order of the day."

The first time I tried it I choked on the "All is well is between us" phrase. But it does get easier and said with less choking noises the more you practice!

Rinse and Repeat for 28 days and it will work for you as it did for me. You may have to revisit it when something happens, usually around the holidays. But this practice will bring the freedom that comes with forgiveness… the freedom to love yourself enough to release the poison called Hatred.

Now that we have used the key of "I Forgive You and I Set Me Free" to unlock us out of Hatred into Forgiveness we can move on to the next chapter for anyone who is stuck in Shame that keeps us unhappy, into Dignity and Happiness.

CHAPTER 5

Out of Shame...into Dignity

Kai: "I wish I had cared more. I wish I had been there for her. I wish I had taken time to help her. I was selfish with my time and attention… and now she's gone and I can't bring her back."

Arlene: "I had a good life. A great job, a beautiful circle of friends and family. I don't know what came over me that day. I didn't see her because I was texting. I hit and killed a child. I will never forgive myself. I want to die. I can't get the sound of my car hitting her out of my head. Please help me."

Sebastian: "I remember her words as if it was yesterday… 'Let me teach you how to make you feel good. And don't tell anyone about our little secret.' I was seven. I didn't know any better and I was scared to tell my mom. She was my mom's friend and my babysitter. When she stopped, I could only have pleasure when I knew it was wrong. I am so ashamed of what I've done to other kids now. I can say I couldn't help myself but that's a lie. I can't help myself. I can't help others. I deserve to die."

Have you said or done something that makes you sick to your stomach? Are you waiting to die to rid yourself of the guilt? Are you numbing yourself with anything that will help you not remember?

Check all that apply:

- ❑ I can't forget
- ❑ I will never be forgiven
- ❑ I deserve to be hated
- ❑ I can't live with the guilt
- ❑ I am so ashamed
- ❑ I will never forgive myself
- ❑ I can't live with this feeling of complete revulsion with myself
- ❑ I can't lose the haunting vision in my head
- ❑ I would give anything, my life, everything to be able to take it back
- ❑ I wish I had never been born
- ❑ I wish I could go back and change everything
- ❑ I will never be able to live this down
- ❑ I deserve to die

Sound Familiar?

Are you in shame from an accident? An assault? A rape? A molestation? Cheating? Bullying? Fraud? Burglary? Murder?

The many faces of shame have one thing in common. They haunt you. They follow you. They rob you of any joy in life. Happiness is a pipe dream.

It's not any easy place to rise again from. Whether it was on purpose or by accident, shame is a deadly virus, deeply rooted, life-killing poison. So, let's start shoveling out the shiitake so we can stop the infection and then turn around and use it as fertilizer to grow the beauty that you are.

Let Me Give You A "Peace" of My Mind

Why do people do bad things? For many and no reason. We try to find relief in answers like genetics, trauma leading to trauma, a birth defect, a lack of moral fiber, a cultural make-up, self-sabotage and as usual… we try to un-confuse an answer-less life question. And so, if you are asking yourself, "Why did I do that? Why do I want to do that? Why am I so damaged? Why am I so screwed up? Why am I tempted to act in dark ways? What is wrong with me?" Try to stop asking the questions. Because the Critic will answer vehemently over and over again with words of shame and blame that will keep you down. "You are hopeless useless and damned." It will use the events to back you into a corner and keep you there. The Sad One will keep you doomed. "I can never make this right so I might as well just give up and give in." There is no way out when the Critic or the Sad One are running the show. But even when we cannot undo what we have said or done, there is a way to happiness out of Shame into Dignity.

Foundation Peace: Exorcising the Past

You can start your life over at any time, as many times as you want. And you can find a new road that doesn't keep you falling into the same shame hole over and over again. And you don't have to spend a lifetime in therapy or take a numbing agent to make it better. But you have to be willing to go into that hole one last time. There's a saying in the 12-step program, "You are only as sick as your secrets" and one of the cornerstone steps is cleaning up the wreckage of your past by being honest about those very things that left alone, develop an infection in your heart and soul. It's time to go dig out the roots of the weeds that are choking the life out of you.

Learning in Action with Balance Tools

Balance Tool: Digging Out the Infected Roots

Take a deep breath, close your eyes and allow yourself to be one with the shame, the regret, the anguish, the horrible ugly memories. It is time to heal… even this.

What happened, exactly, where is the root of the shame? This is a private 'for your eyes only' exercise. Leave nothing out. We will decide later what we'll do with it… your job is to be thorough no matter how painful it might be… if you can, go to the beach to do this so you can be supported and enveloped by the Ocean of Abundance and Mother Nature

Complete the entire story, the true story of what happened as you remember it…

Who was there?

_____

_____

_____

_____

When did it happen?

_____

_____

_____

_____

Where did it happen?

_____

_____

_____

_____

What events led up to it happening?

_____

_____

_____

What happened?

_____

_____

_____

_____

Now as you are writing, the voices in your head might be going crazy, so let's identify them and invite them to have a seat and rest so you can complete the exercise. Here are the Belief Systems (BS) that keep us suffering when we are stuck in shame.

The Critic:

"You really screwed up."

"How could you have done that?!"

"What the hell were you thinking?"

"Sorry is not good enough."

"There's no forgiveness for what you did."

"You'll have to pay for this for the rest of your life."

"You might as well end it now."

"You're damaged."

"There's no redemption for you."

The Brat:

"It wasn't my fault, if they hadn't said/done what they did, I wouldn't have done them wrong."

"They started it."

"Why is it always my fault?"

"It's NOT my fault"

"Screw you."

The Sad One:

"I am so ashamed."

"I am so sorry but sorry isn't enough."

"I am a sad excuse for a human being."

"There's no hope for me."

"Just let me go away forever."

All of these statements from your Critic, Brat and Sad One keep you in the shadow of shame. They are lies.

Soothe them with words from your Balanced Center Self...

"Thank you very much for the input, but you are not telling the whole truth. The truth is that everything that happens is for me to learn grow and expand from. I have a birthright to live a happy life 88% of the time. There is nothing that cannot be forgiven. I have been forgiven. I can forgive myself. Critic, have a seat you must be very tired...you sound like a broken record. And I appreciate that you think you are helping...but you're NOT!"

Now, you can affirm the Balanced Truth spoken from your Balanced Center Self:

- Since there's no do-overs, I have no choice, I have to accept what I did/said.
- Yes, I made a mistake.
- I did something at the time which I wish I didn't.
- I did/said something that at the time that was the best I could do in those circumstances.
- I am truly sorry.
- If I had a do-over I would make different choices.

- I cannot go back.
- But I can move forward making a living amends.
- I want to feel better.
- I will feel better about this.
- This missed-take in the drama of my life is not my whole life.
- I not a mistake.
- I am not a horrible person.
- I am not damned to hell.
- I am not good for nothing.
- I am 88 percent good for everything.
- I can and will stop beating myself up.
- I am not broken. I can make a new start now.
- I can strengthen my muscle to act on my own behalf.

☯ Balance Tool: Disinfecting the Past

We human beings have a conscience. Whether we are brought up in a church, with strict parents or not, we have an inner guidance system that tells us when we are off... that tells us if we have strayed off the path of the kind, good, whole sentient beings that we are naturally. So, in order to move from Shame to Dignity, we have to act on our own behalf and develop esteem through esteemable acts. Now that you've written down the whole truth and nothing but the truth, it's time to pay your own piper.

Similar to the Forgiveness exercise in the last chapter, this requires a 'rinse and repeat.' For the next 28 days:

Sit quietly in a favorite spot. If you can get to a beach or by water all the better as the healing energy there is powerful.

Take a breath.

Ask your Balanced Centered Self the following questions and just write down whatever comes into your heart and mind.

What can I do to make an amends?

_____

_____

_____

_____

_____

_____

_____

What can I say that shows sincere remorse?

_____

_____

_____

_____

_____

_____

I can prove that I am sorry through the following actions…

_____

_____

_____

_____

_____

_____

I can make a living amends by changing my…

_____

_____

_____

_____

_____

_____

_____

I can start with a letter of I'm sorry to all of those affected… I don't have to decide right now whether to send it or not.

I'm Sorry

_____

_____

_____

_____

_____

_____

_____

If you have already tried to make amends to say sorry prior to this moment and the words were not acknowledged or accepted that's okay.

This exercise is for you first…not for them. As part as my living amends I can just allow them to have their reaction, no matter how horrible it might feel to me. I cannot take it back, and they have the right to feel badly. I will take care of my side of the street so that I feel okay about me.

Whatever it was you did or said, it was done, yes, and you cannot unring a bell. But you can move on, you can clean up your past, and you have a way to Happiness with the following truth:

- We are all precious creations in a Friendly Universe.
- Everything happens for our Divine and Best Good.
- We are all connected to each other to bring out the best in each other, even when the interaction might be painful at times.
- You are not the sum a few bad decisions. You are not perfect. You can forgive yourself for this.
- You are forgiven by a Friendly Universe.
- You are Loving Loved and Lovable.
- Your do-over can begin right now.
- You can clean up your past.
- You can start again and be a Beneficial Presence on the Planet.
- There one billion good, kind, wonderful, beautiful acts you can engage in now for the rest of your life.
- You can start now.
- It is your choice.

Rise above your Shame. Find your way to Dignity through your Shame. Life is too short to punish yourself into Eternity. You are wrapped in a warm blanket of worthiness no matter what… now do the healing work that you deserve.

CHAPTER 6

Out of Fear...into Freedom

Are you a worrywart? Are you afraid much of the time? Are you waiting for the other shoe to drop? Then this chapter is just for you!

CHECK ALL THAT APPLY:

- ❑ I am barely making it.
- ❑ What if I get laid off too?
- ❑ What if I lose my investments?
- ❑ What if I can't pay my mortgage?
- ❑ What if I lose my house?
- ❑ What if I can't pay rent?
- ❑ I'm afraid.
- ❑ I will fail.
- ❑ I tried that already.
- ❑ I tried that already and it didn't work.
- ❑ I can't risk it.
- ❑ What if I fall on my face?
- ❑ What if I am humiliated again?
- ❑ What if I lose?
- ❑ What if I lose my job?
- ❑ What if she leaves me?
- ❑ What if I get sick?

- ❑ What if my family gets hurt?
- ❑ What if my kids die before I do?
- ❑ What if we all die in a nuclear war?
- ❑ It makes me sick to my stomach thinking about it.
- ❑ My heart races so much I think I'm going to drop dead of a heart attack.
- ❑ I can't breathe.
- ❑ I don't have what it takes.
- ❑ No matter what I do, it will never be enough.
- ❑ No matter how much I achieve, the joy is short-lived, if at all.
- ❑ No matter how hard I try, it doesn't come out right.
- ❑ I am tired of trying.
- ❑ There's no point in trying anymore.
- ❑ I am in a cage and there's no way out.

Sound Familiar?

John: Fear. Anxiety. Panic. I am afraid to try, afraid not to try, afraid of people places and situations. I am so messed up. I really want to be brave and then I try and I just can't. My mouth dries up. My stomach turns. My chest tightens. I feel like I'm going to suffocate. My heart beats harder and faster and harder and faster until I think I am just going to pop like a balloon that is blown up too much. I've tried medication and I feel like I'm walking through molasses. Where does my fear come from? Why am I so screwed up? Please help me.

In this chapter of Freedom, you are about to embark on a process, if you are willing, to come face to face with Fear… fear that comes from past pain, fear that comes from BS Belief Systems that keep you disconnected, and fear from the ego controlling your mind. It's time to address the fear that keeps you afraid of life, that keeps you afraid of being yourself, and afraid of being fully alive. It's time to face the fear that keeps you behind bars without freedom to choose happiness.

Mike: I feel like I'm sitting on a high diving board, paralyzed, just holding on, looking down to the cement below, past the rungs of the ladder that I've climbed up thus far in life, from achievement to achievement, relationship to relationship, success to success, failure to failure, disappointment to disappointment. And I'm tired and feeling more and more hopeless exhausted, and alone. Every once in a while, I am tempted by the thought of jumping onto the cement below, just to stop the anguish I feel in my heart and the confusion and dis-ease in my head.

This chapter work that we are about to do together will take you on a trip back into your life, and relook at the journey from a different perspective, so that you can let go, and realize that you are only one foot from the cement and will land safely and that there really is nothing to be afraid of. You will stand at that edge, take a deep breath and dive into the past, for the last time, to see all things anew, with a pair of Balanced goggles, and then burst to the surface with a magnificent breath of life and love that fills you up with the wonder of being alive. Then, with Balance flippers and instructions on how to reach for the other side, you will swim with grace and ease into the wonder of the Ocean of Abundance also known as the rest of your life. Are you ready?

Let Me Give You A "Peace" of My Heart

Here's a picture of my own Journey from Fear to Freedom. See the bird sitting on a perch in a cage. She looks out yearningly through the slats of her cage. Each bar has a name or place inscribed on it. A camera zooms in on one of the bars. It says Mom. Yes, that one hurt. Three decades ago, it broke one of her wings. Another bar says Husband. Yes, there are bald spots on her wings when she was neglected for years. First, she couldn't fly. Flying was so difficult when she was young. She pushed herself for years and willed herself to fly. Now older she's afraid to fly again. Freedom is a pipe dream. Each bar keeps her from moving forward. People hurt her so badly, her wings ache so much that she can never hope to fly again. The pain, hurt and fear keep her in her cage of loneliness and isolation. I was that wounded bird, longing to fly, longing for someone to set me free. So, I started looking for freedom in all the wrong places:

> To Accomplishments: If I just got the award for youngest to get a degree, I would be free to feel good enough. If I won a beauty contest, I would feel free to say that my mom was wrong, I wasn't fat ugly and clumsy. If I got the most clients in the firm and made the most partners happy, I would be good enough. If I could get people to say, "Is there anything you can't do?" then I would know I was free to relax and stop accomplishing. After three decades of accomplishments, I was not free. In fact, I was on a hamster wheel, constantly busy-busy-busy-exhausted.

> To the Perfect man: If I could just find someone to complete me, and love me for who I am exactly as I am, and not cheat on me, and not ignore me, and pay attention to me, and want me… then I would be free to live and enjoy my life.

> To a Good time: If I could just keep being the belle of the ball, and out-drink and out-party my friends, be the most fun, the most adventurous, the most fascinating with a little help from drugs and alcohol… then I would be free to live and enjoy my life.

> To looking good: If I could just have the nicest house on the block, drive the snazziest car, have the best designer clothes and accessories, have the latest technology, have everything that everyone wants but doesn't have and I can bask in the greenery of envy from others… then I would be free to live and enjoy my life.

Inside my head I was trapped in a crazy cage of fear, anxiety, worry, shame, blame, no-can-do, bitterness, "woulda-shoulda-coulda" regret, and every single action or inaction was fuel for more craziness. There was no rest, no peace, no sigh of relief. Life became a life sentence, trapped, with no way out.

Let's go back to my bird in the cage. Trapped, right? Not necessarily. When the the camera pans back and we see the total picture, there are no bars behind the bird. There is freedom to fly. There is a way out of the cage. There is nothing behind her to keep her inside. All she has to do is turn around.

That is freedom. Turn around. Here's how I did it and you can too.

Let Me Give You A "Peace" of My Mind

First of all, it is okay to feel fear. It's a natural human feeling that helps keep us out of harm's way. But many of us are trapped in fear… fear from our past, fear of our present, and fear of the future. One in four Americans take anti-anxiety and/or antidepressants to try to alleviate their fear… and outside of the side-effects they're feeling, their fear remains. So, what are you afraid of? Let's illuminate the underlying levers in our hearts and minds with my Balance Flashlight, and understand what and who keeps our Fear in the ON position past its usefulness.

Foundation Peace: Fear from our Past

For many, fear began as a protective habit from a dangerous past. In Chapter 4: From Hatred to Forgiveness, I talk about the statistic about the number of kids raised in dysfunctional homes. Ranging from 70% and as high as 93% at the time of this writing, that's a lot of messed up minds! It's no wonder so many people have swollen and heightened fear…fear of violence, fear of abandonment, fear of neglect, fear of being alone, fear of failure, fear of life. And for many "successful people," we've learned how to ignore, perform over and repress that natural fear that developed as a result of our childhood… until we can't keep it under wraps anymore.

Many of us built rafts to help us navigate the treacherous whitewater rapids that threatened to drown us as kids. Children who have been abused develop an over-sensitivity, and/or a hardened shell to protect themselves. We construct walls of control to keep the enemy out… that unfortunately we also keep the love out as well. Abuse and neglect also create many a workaholic, or other kinds of addiction that keep the painful feelings and memories at bay. The heavy rafts help us maneuver the whitewater until we are adults, but then around mid-life, we begin to buckle under the weight of the raft. We carry it around 'just in case' there's more danger, but as an adult we are not physically in danger anymore… we can defend against violators, but we still carry the emotional fear which is the heavy raft that becomes a burden to carry. Many of my clients make it to what I call midlife opportunity instead of midlife crisis, when a pressure panel pops off and the overflow of fear and anxiety flood them in their tracks. Others never find a way out of fear from the start and are lost in the deep end of the life pool.

> *Esther*: I kicked butt. I was always the fastest, smartest, brightest and prettiest. Until now. I am afraid of everything and everyone. I don't know what happened. And day by day I care less about what is going to happen. I've gone to therapy, I'm taking prescription drugs and I don't feel any better.

I worked with Esther using the concepts and the exercises from Chapter 4: Out of Hatred into Forgiveness and after some digging she revealed that her childhood was less than optimal. She hated her mother, who was narcissistic and had basically left her to raise herself. Esther began developing a protective shell of denial and an "I don't care" attitude that lent itself well in her high-powered world of high finance workaholic environment. It wasn't until she had her own child that her past pain and fear that she was not allowed to feel as a child came up and bit her in the butt. She had built a raft to navigate the dangerous waters of her time alone as a child as an overachiever. But now that heavy raft of working 80 hours a week and pushing herself to the limits had its downside… because now when there was no dangerous whitewater around, no reason to feel alone and abandoned, she was still carrying the protective raft which was getting heavier and heavier. Adding a child to her already heavy load was the last straw and she buckled under. Fear ruled her life and the side effects from the anti-anxiety drugs were leading to suicidal thoughts. But without the drugs, the levels of anxiety was debilitating and kept Esther from being able to function in her day to day activities caring for her daughter. I am happy to say that she is now medication free and uses her cadre of Balance tools to sooth her fear away and enjoy her new family immensely.

Past pain will keep you in a state of fear whether you are conscious of it or not. If you relate to Esther's experience, try using the Balance Tool: Feeling Past Pain Fully from Chapters 3: Out of Heartbreak into Love and Balance Tools: Forgiving Mothers and insert Fathers or Teachers or Family or whomever the repressed anger is towards along with The Forgiveness Exercise from Chapter 4: Out of Hatred into Forgiveness. However, some of us are not so much afraid from our past but as worry warts, we are afraid of what the future may bring.

Foundation Peace: Future Fear and Faith

So, what are you afraid of? Let's look under the bed with my Balance Flashlight.

- That I won't have any money left when I retire
- That I will end up homeless
- That I will be hurt emotionally, physically, mentally
- That my family will be hurt emotionally, physically, mentally
- That I will die early
- That I will get sick
- That my family will suffer a tragedy
- *Add your own here…*
- _____

- _____

- _____

- _____

Living in Fear has become a habit for many people, especially Americans. As I mentioned in Chapter 4, one in four Americans are on anti-anxiety and/or antidepressant medication. And it's ironic because we are supposedly one of the richest countries in the world with limitless opportunities and even called the Land of the Free. So why are we so afraid? And why are we so unhappy? *Psychology Today* and *Fortune* magazine state that Americans are more than twice as affluent as we were 55 years ago, but we are at all time high levels of life dissatisfaction.

I believe that one of the main underpinnings of fear comes from believing that evil will overtake good. And the news certainly helps fueling that battle. The media is a master fear instigator, I'm sure you've heard of the expression "if it bleeds, it leads". Michael Bernard Beckwith calls the media a weapon of mass distraction! Of course, we will be afraid when all we see is the worst in people… war, rape, murder, theft, terror, tragedy and catastrophe. We are lucky if we get one feel good story a day.

Fear is a natural reaction if you think that life is random, meaningless, disconnected and unfriendly. That our only goal in life is to make as much money so that we can buy toys and have enough to retire on, and that when bad things happen, it's just proof that the Universe is unfriendly. Life is about waking up every day trying to dodge a bullet so that we won't have anything tragic happen to us or those in our family circle. I believe that I am entitled to a fulfilled happy life, which means that there should be no pain, and when there is, I've either had bad luck or bad karma or both.

In this BS Belief System, you will be a natural worry-wart, living each day in a worst-case scenario otherwise known as FEAR: Future Events Already Ruined. I guarantee that worry is 100% negatively correlated with Happiness. Worry is 100% positively correlated to Fear. So, what's the way out of Fear into Freedom?

It's time to "put the moose on the table," which is an expression I came up with to replace "the elephant in the room," since I was born in Canada! Yes, it's time to have a "come to Jesus talk" but not literally. It's time to drop the G bomb. Yes, God, Source, Allah, Jesus, Krishna, Creator, Yahweh, Spirit, whatever you want to call that Power that is Great and Greater than the past, pain, and future fear. If you really want to move from Fear to Freedom, it helps to believe that there is something more meaningful than just random human beings banging around together on the Planet. Why?

If I choose to believe in nothingness, in chaos, in random, then I feel uneasy, disconnected, uncomfortable, meaningless, and I go directly to Fear… no 'pass go,' just directly behind the bars of the Jail called Fear, again. Since I am really alone on the planet with no one to fend for me except me, I have to be hyper-vigilant and in a constant state of fearful readiness to guard against anything bad happening.

I could also believe in an angry God who needs anger management classes, which would also keep me in fear. I actually grew up in a fundamental religion and had a difficult time with what I saw as hypocritical dogma. I could not accept that my beloved grandfather, who refused to follow the rules, was, as a result, damned to hell. I actually went to a religious school and flunked out because I had too many questions. So, I proudly flashed my atheist card. It wasn't until my marriage fell apart and I found temporary comfort in a bottle that I had to revisit the question of God or a Power outside of myself. Because without a belief in something greater than me, I was screwed, because I knew I wasn't God, and that if I was all there was, I was in trouble! So, in my spiritual experience with Batman, that I described in Chapter One, I had my antidote to Fear. I have nothing to fear because I choose to believe in the Greater Good which connects us all. I choose Faith over Fear.

So, the billion-dollar question is… is living in Fear working for you? You can choose to stay in pain, anger, righteous indignation, guilt, worry, blame, shame, bitterness, envy… that's easy. No effort is required to stay on the same path that you're accustomed to… it's normal, the way it is, the way we deserve, the way we're used to. And your choice. If you have been marinating in fear, it will be easier to just stay there. It's a habit now. But here's some good news. Habits can be changed!

But, Dr. Marissa, you say, it's not that easy. Yes and no. Choice is my most powerful Life Tool. Choice gifts me the Freedom to Focus and believe in what I want to. I am Free to believe that there's a balance between the Santa God and the Angry God, a balance between self-sufficiency and self-imprisoned isolation, and an informed alliance with the Power that created the planets, the oceans, the beauty of all creatures, including us. I am Free to believe that we are not separate from this Power but that we are a natural wonderful extension of Life in all of its glory and wonder. I am Free to believe that we all come to this planet to find, hone, and play with our unique talents and abilities, which is God expressing through us. I am Free to celebrate my uniqueness, free to see life as a Joyride with lots of stops to get off at to explore. And you are Free to choose that too!

And why am I trying to get you to drink this Kool-Aid? Simply, because it feels better! When I choose to believe in a Power that we are all connected to that is responsible for creating Life, I feel powerful and light and as Esther Hicks says, "Frisky... I feel tuned in, tapped in, and turned on". I feel hopeful, optimistic, positive, energized, fun-loving, funny, smiley and free to laugh, create and play. So really, the choice is yours. It can be that simple. You can choose to live in Fear or you can choose to Free yourself to live in Limitlessness. Again, as Abraham says through Esther, "We humans are so free, we are free to choose bondage." And that is what Fear is... bondage, a trap that we can choose for ourselves, or not.

In order to turn away from Fear and towards Freedom, one must develop a different set of muscles, mind-body-spirit-soul muscles. Turning requires the use of peripheral vision, to believe in a Greater Good acting and conspiring on your own behalf. In Neale Donald Walsch's classic *Conversations with God* series, we understand that the Source or God or the Friendly Universe is always sending messages of Joy, Truth, and Love. Because we have free will, it's up to us to tune in or not. If I deny the existence of God, it will be a lonely and random place for me. In order to tune in to K-LIFE, I have to choose to change my station. Because I choose to believe in a Friendly Universe, or God, or Source, or as I call Him, my UPS Man: my Universal Power Source Who Delivers more and more Good, as long as I stay at my address, I am not tuned in to K-FEAR.

We can choose to see pain as a purifier, a chiseling as I described with my Rock story in Chapter Four. When bad things do happen, we can choose to know that everything is going to be Okay in the end, and if it's not Okay, it's not the end. We can choose to see the opportunity that comes with loss. We can find the blessing in the mess. We can choose to take the path Halle Berry shared in my Red Carpet interview with her: "If you're going through hell… keep going." We can ask ourselves what is trying to emerge when our hearts break open in tragedy. And when I am tempted to worry or dip my toe into fear, I remember that "Worry is a Prayer for bad things to happen," a Native American saying. And His Holiness the Fourteenth Dalai Lama agrees with me with "If there's a problem and there's a solution, there's nothing to worry about, and if there's a problem and there's no solution, there's still nothing to worry about!"

I have nothing to fear in this lifetime. I know that I am going to die. But death does not mean the end, as I discussed in Chapter Two. It's just a transition, because I choose to believe life is eternal. When someone close to me gets hurt, I am sad and mad and then I tune myself back into Faith and Freedom, talk shows on my K-Life Radio channel that restore my ability to feel good again. I choose to feel all of the feelings that come with being alive… to find the gift in the present, to choose to leave behind past pain, to choose to ignore future fear. And you can choose that too. Breathe.

Learning in Action with Balance Tools

Balance Tool: Connection through Meditation

The most effective way to reinforce our connection to a Friendly Universe is to spend a little time each day connecting with that Energy. Many people call this practice meditation, which is a little different than prayer. The simplest way I understand the distinction is that prayer is asking for something and meditation is just receiving or listening. Meditation can also be as complicated or as simple as you choose to make it. If you like structure and variety, there are a myriad of methods for meditation. For simplicity, I am going to share just two kinds, still and moving meditation.

Still meditation is just that… you are still and you try to still your mind from thoughts, which have a tendency to lead you down a thinking rabbit trail… sometimes like Hansel and Gretel, including losing the bread crumbs back to safety.

Still meditation doesn't require any specific mantra or seated position, although there's nothing wrong with practices that advocate them. I do recommend that you start small and not criticize yourself no matter what you are able to do or not do. I ask my clients to start with a two-minute timer and just focus on their breath…In… and Out… In… and Out.

If you have a thought like "this is stupid", "this is a waste of my time", "I'm going to be late", just breathe in the thought and then release it in the out breath. Some of my clients like counting to stop thought and breathe in on "One" and out on "Two" and so on. When they find themselves meandering off on a thought, no problem; just start counting over. And One-One-One is just fine. Every day you can add a minute until a maximum of 15 minutes. I believe that there's too much life to live to sit for hours, but that's just me. If you maintain this practice, or "blissipline," as Michael Bernard Beckwith calls it, one day you'll realize that you actually just naturally love doing it, and I promise it will happen! Wise teacher Abraham through Esther Hicks recommends meditation as an important way to still the mind so that any resistant thoughts or feelings that contradict the love that is constantly beaming out to us melt away. I love Deepak Chopra's analogy in his book *7 Spiritual Laws of Success* that in meditation, sometimes our minds are in so much turmoil with thought that if the Empire State Building fell in, it wouldn't make a splash! In the book, *Eat Pray Love*" by Elizabeth Gilbert, one of my favorite lines is "In meditation, my thought patterns are known so well now that they don't bother me anymore… they've become like old neighbors, kind of bothersome but ultimately rather endearing… Mr. and Mrs. Yakkity Yak and their 3 dumb children, blah blah and blah… there's room for us all in this neighborhood."

Some of you might be saying "But Dr. Marissa, I've tried to meditate and I can't sit still!" Good news, moving meditation will be perfect for you and I am quite liberal with my definition. I consider yoga and Chinese yoga, aka Balance Tai Qi Qong which I teach (sorry, couldn't resist the commercial) to be moving meditation as well as jogging, hiking, swimming, walking, skating, skiing. Any time you are focused on an activity more than you are on the thoughts running through your head, I consider it a moving meditation. Try to worry less about the semantics and just try it. It's is the best way to strengthen your connection with a Friendly Universe.

I meditate every day. My UPS Man, my Universal Power Source delivers every morning when I meditate on the beach. Choosing that moniker has a side benefit… I am constantly reminded how All Present my Source is because I get to see UPS trucks go by all day, and inevitably they always shows up when I have an inspired thought or question. One day I wasn't feeling very supported on the way to a client site where my project was in danger of being cancelled. I pulled up to the light on San Vicente and I swear, there was a UPS truck in front of me, and then two more pulled up on both sides of me and then one behind me… as if to say, "I Got You".

Now that we've covered how to move from Fear of the Future to Freedom in Faith, let's take a look at another underlying lever of Fear that resides in the Present, with the Ego's constant chatter that keeps us tense and unhappy.

Foundation Peace: Free from the Fear to be Me

Mark: I tried to stand out and excel. I succeeded and received a lot of accolades throughout my school years and on the job. But with every compliment I would outwardly say, "Thank you," and inwardly I was afraid. Fear that I would get found out. Fear that someday someone would find out that I'm not as great as they think I am. Fear that I am really not good enough… that I am not lovable enough to be loved.

Some of my clients do not have memories of a bad childhood; they remember loving friends and family and supportive parents. Regardless, a pervasive feeling of not being good enough or smart enough or impending doom seems to plague them. I actually have noticed this phenomenon after presenting at Career Days for the past 15 years at my daughters' schools. I ask kids of all ages about the 'voices in their heads'… in particular, the one that says, "you're not good enough, you're not thin enough, you're not pretty enough" and about the age of 10, this voice seems to show up… regardless of how happy or unhappy their home life was. We could wonder if it is society's standards that are broadcast in the media, which plants the "less than others" comparison, or it could be something picked up in peer pressure, or just part of being in the human race, where race naturally means winning and losing, better and worse. Whatever the reason, and there may be multiple points of blame; that voice seems to be the culprit for overly critical self-consciousness and the development of low self-esteem, which feeds Fear.

This chatter in the head is usually the voice of the Ego, and the Ego is self-centered and uses fear to protect itself. Just listen to what goes on in your head on a regular basis. At the low end of the spectrum, experts estimate that the mind thinks on average between 50,000 and 60,000 thoughts per day, which means about 2100 thoughts per hour. And out of the 60,000, about 56,400 are regarding **_our_** own needs. Yes, ego is extremely self-centered.

Here's an excerpt from my crazy head on a day driving to the gym… and we'll take a listen to all of the voices in the committee whom you are now well acquainted with who are also different facets of my ego.

> Agnes, my Inner Brat: "Wow, that woman should be working out here at the gym every day!"

> Rose, my Inner Critic: "Well you should talk… you look like a bag of potatoes… no wonder your wasband told everyone you were obese. You should park over there and walk and start your workout before you get inside."

Agnes the Brat: Upon eyeing the front desk staff…"Don't they have "practice what we preach" standards for people who work here? I hope he will be using his free membership to lose some weight. Maybe they are going to be 'before and after' examples." "Wow, I am glad I don't look like her."

Rose the Critic: "Have you taken a good look in the mirror lately? You have no right to talk, lady."

Agnes the Brat: "Oh there's that guy again. If I looked like that I would definitely put a shirt on. I wish I was a guy. To walk around completely oblivious would be fun once in awhile. Oh, there's that angry woman. If I looked like her I'd be angry, too!"

Sarah the Sad One: "Sigh, I wish I looked like her. I used to…"

Rose the Critic: "Yes you did look like that but you really let yourself go. That's why you are alone. No one will ever find your body attractive. Such flab… good thing you wear nice clothes… but you know it's really false advertising. As soon as you take them off, any man would take off screaming!"

Sound familiar? It used to be said that if you heard voices in your head, you are crazy. I am here to tell you that if you don't identify the different voices and address them, you will go crazy.

Our internal Brat keeps us thinking we are Hot Shiitake: "I look better than you, I am smarter than you, I feel sorry for you, and I'm glad I'm not like you. I'm better than you and full of myself." On the other hand, our internal Critic keeps us feeling like a Piece of Shiitake: "No matter what I do, I step in fear, failure, worthlessness and good for nothingness. No matter how much success I have, no matter how many people tell me how great I am, it's never enough. In the end, people will find out how awful I really am and be sick of me.

The swing from one end of this pendulum to the other extreme is exhausting. I just have to listen to myself talk in my head for two minutes to want to jump out the window. One of my favorite quotes from the 12-step program is, "My mind is like a dangerous neighborhood, you don't want to go in there alone." One of my own favorites is, "I think, therefore I am screwed" or "At night, when I take off my bra and jewelry… I wish I could take my head off, too, and set it on the nightstand!"

And this chatter comes from all sides of the Ego. Ego is the bondage of Self and keeps us in fear and without freedom. The ego is very powerful and wants us to be hyper-vigilant for all manner of attack. It is the voice in my head that feeds on fear, that tells me I should always be on the watch, careful, just in case someone tries to hurt me, punish me, neglect me, disrespect me, embarrass me, or dishonor me. It will bring up a slideshow of all the hurts from the past, all those who have done me wrong.

Ego is also the Critic voice that says "Nothing good is good enough, so you better hustle some more. That was good, but if you don't keep piling up those certificates, people will see that you aren't really all that, so let's show them some more. And if things are going well, it's just a matter of time before the other shoe will drop. So, keep striving, doing, achieving, buying, showing, standing, bowing, rushing, planning, pushing, pushing, pushinnnnng." This side of my ego I've named Rose the Critic. Yup you already know it's my mom's name!

And if someone is unhappy with you, the streetcar named Ego swings you from one end of the track: "I am a piece of shiitake on the pavement called humiliation," which is the Critic to the other end, "How dare you be critical of me…you are not the boss of me, what right do you have, who do you think you are, and I don't need you so Eff you!" which is the Brat end of the Ego. It tells us that we are special, better than others, deserving of the best…that we are too good for most people places and things. That we need to be worshipped and honored and that we must do things perfectly and be all things to all people at all times… exhausting, and never enough.

And if that isn't enough head banging, there's another front that the Critic part of our Ego likes to launch an attack on… we are conditioned to feel ashamed if we are "full of ourselves," if we are selfish and self-centered and self-absorbed, and the list goes on. So, when someone says, "I want to find myself," or "I need to take care of myself," or "I need to think of myself more," there is a thick string attached that says, "Whoa, Nelly, don't get ahead of yourself! You're sounding like a narcissist and that's a no-no."

However, I do have to interject here and stand up for the Ego before we do any more character assassination. I am grateful for my Ego because it did protect me in the dangerous waters of my past. If it were not for the critical and bratty voices in my head when I was being beaten as a child, I might already be dead. My Ego helped me navigate those dangerous white-water messages that I was fat ugly and clumsy, it helped keep me safe with habits and protection that just don't serve me well now. So, I do thank Rose and Agnes who represent the two extremes of my ego… I just tell them that it's time for a vacation… they don't have to work so hard anymore. Balanced Centered Marissa is getting stronger every day and we don't have to live in fear anymore. Now that we're clear about where the roots of our fear sprout from, we can recalibrate with some Balance tools to strengthen our Balanced Centered voice and quiet down the Ego.

Balance Tool: L'eggo of My Ego so I Can be Free to be Me

So, what does free to be me mean? It means avoiding both extremes… the egomaniac "hot shiitake" and the codependent "piece of shiitake." Sometimes, in an effort to avoid being selfish or full of ourselves, we overcompensate to codependency, where "I think so little of myself that I am not just a doormat, I am wall-to-wall carpet!" My mother's, my child's, my partner's, my bosses', my 'anyone other than me' needs are more important than my own so that my life is spent constantly trying to please them until there is nothing left of me. That can be as harmful as the egomaniac. I keep myself centered when I remember what my priority order is… God, Self, Others. God as in my connection with Source/UPS Man, then loving myself and then loving others. In other words, understanding that we are not Hot Shiitake AND we are not a Piece of Shiitake… we are just pretty good shiitake!

Balance Tool: The Insulting Game

Here's a great exercise that helps free us from the bondage of Self and Ego. It's taking what our ego fears most…to be insulted, humiliated, abhorred, put down and actually make fun of it!

Take a breath. Take your pen or sit at your computer and ask your Critic to help you list EVERY single insult you've ever received in your lifetime. I know, it sounds horrible but I promise it will be okay. We will balance our way out of the shiitake but first we have to come face to face with the shiitake. And just so you feel better, I will start with mine. And these are not made up insults in my head… these are ones people have actually said and we shrivel remembering, and we replay them over and over and over and over again. That replay allows the ego to defend itself and keeps the wall up between ourselves and the freedom to be loving loved and lovable. So, the walls are coming down NOW!!

> You're UGLY!
> You're so full of yourself!
> You're FAT!
> You've let yourself go!
> You're OBESE!
> Who do you think you are?!
> You're such a self-promoter!
> You are disgusting (I'm not sure if someone actually said this or my Internal Critic made it up but I'm putting it down just in case)
> You are not as pretty as you think you are.
> You are not in the same league as they are.
> You are small-time.
> You're really not that important.
> You are such a hypocrite.
> You are sooooo sensitive.
> You think you are all that but you are not.
> You need to look for a guy that is at your own level, hot guys wouldn't be attracted to you.
> You put yourself on a pedestal (that was last week).
> You act like you are better than other people and you're not.
> I would rather chew glass than listen to another one of Dr. Pei's lectures.
> OUCH OUCH OUCH OUCH!!

But actually, when I was doing this exercise I started to laugh inside, and then out. Yes, people can be so cruel and at the same time, sticks and stones can break my bones but names will not hurt me. Why? Because I have a Balanced Centered Self that is strong enough to own the truth which is in the middle of the sticks and stones.

I know how wonderful I am 88% of the time. I have unique gifts, qualities, and abilities and at the same time, I can overdo those abilities. And I am not perfect. And so, freedom to be me means that I can own all of me...the good the bad and the beautiful. I can own the insults today... maybe not in the moment that they are hurled but certainly after a little meditation time or soothing time. Now that I have all of the uglies out in front of me, I can deal with them in the same way that we have been in prior chapters. My Balanced Center Self has a loving response for each and every one that finds the middle between the Critic's Response, the Brat's Response and the Sad One's Response.

Let me illustrate:

> Critic Rose: "You're UGLY! You are not as pretty as you think you are. You are not in the same league as they are. You need to look for a guy that is at your own level, hot guys wouldn't be attracted to you."

> Balanced Centered Marissa: "Sweetheart, that's not true. You are beautiful. Yes, that boy on the bike did say that all those years ago, but he was wrong. You are beautiful in my eyes and many others. How many times have you been told you're beautiful? Many, many, many times... one ugly remark to probably a hundred thousand. So, you can let that one go."

> Critic Rose: "You're so full of yourself! Who do you think you are?! You're such a self-promoter! You are small time. You're really not that important. You think you are all that but you are not. You put yourself on a pedestal. You act like you are better than other people and you're not."

Balanced Centered Marissa: "Well you can be sometimes… that's true. It takes courage to step out and do what you do… to constantly offer up yourself and step out and step forward without knowing if it's safe or not… so you do have to have a little bit of an inflated ego to do that. I know you are much less confident than you appear to be to others, and I know that you want to fold in when people hurl insults at you, but it's really okay…it is a combination of where they are, they may be jealous, they may not like you and they also may be right. But that fullness that looks like bragging that may offend people is just part of who you are. Nothing to be ashamed or angry about. Yes, Agnes Brat you can say, "How Dare They" and get all mad because you have always been nice to them and have never said anything mean to them, but they are just expressing their opinion. You can let them express, you don't have to take it on as an attack… it's just their opinion. And Rose Critic, yes, you have heard this opinion and criticism before so maybe there's some holding back we need to do, but it's still only three comments versus hundreds of thousands who have expressed loving appreciation for who you are in the fullness of who you are and more. So, let's not let the three uglies cancel out the 100,000 beauties. And darling, the fact of the matter is, you do have a gift with words, and a gift of healing and helping that is your unique talent so don't bow your head. Smile, breathe and step into the spotlight like you know how to do! And also, remember what your big brother, Michael Bernard Beckwith, always says… when you stop being mediocre and walk in the light of your gifts, you will piss people off! Well, that might not be exactly what he says from the pulpit, but you get the drift!"

Critic Rose: "You're FAT! You've let yourself go! You're OBESE! You are disgusting."

Sad Sarah: "I will always be fat and I just want to hide"

Balanced Centered Marissa: "Darling, you've struggled with your weight since you were 10. That was about the time that you knew that the beatings you were getting were wrong, but you couldn't do anything to change it except rebel by eating. Every time your mom called you fat ugly and clumsy, and pinched you and kicked you under the table, you were so angry and mad and sad that you did the only thing that made you feel better… you would go down after everyone was asleep and sneak food out of the fridge. That's when it all started and it was your coping device and it's okay… you were hurting. And then you starved yourself because you wanted to be admired and whistled at to prove that your mom was wrong… that you couldn't be ugly if you were able to model! And you did model successfully and you are beautiful and you are a sight for sore eyes and you are pretty enough. You have nothing to prove anymore, sweetheart. It doesn't matter that you don't fit into your 'post-divorce down 40 pounds' clothes. It doesn't matter that you don't look like you did when you were modeling. You look like you. Right now. And I am so proud of you for going to the gym to swim even when you don't feel like it, and not eating unhealthy food most of the time, and not obsessing but being careful at the same time, and taking suggestions and trying different things, and most of all working on yourself so that you can love your body and your size and your mind and your heart. You are doing the best that you can with the time that you have and the resources you've been given. The extra weight will drop off slowly and in the meantime, there are plenty of guys who think your body is HOT!"

Rose Critic: "You are such a hypocrite."

Balanced Centered Marissa: "Yes, that's true… not all of the time but every once in awhile, I mess up and do NOT practice what I teach… why do you think I named my talk show, "Take

My Advice, I'm Not Using It"! But most of the time, 88% of the time I do practice what I teach, and 'What you think of me is none of my business!!' I learned that from another one of my guests, Dr. Terry Cole-Whittaker, who has a mega-bestselling book with that title."

Rose Critic: "You are so sensitive!!!"

Balanced Centered Marissa: "I heard this my entire childhood growing up and it would send me to the moon!! But the reality is that it is true! And, of course, I would be, with the kind of angry cruel words hurled at me over and over and over again. There was no time between insults to blister into hardened skin, like guitar fingers. So my sensitivity stayed heightened. And now I've actually come full circle because, I am super glad that I am sensitive… because the research is showing that there is a high correlation between sensitivity and creativity… and who doesn't want that?"

Rose Critic: "I would rather chew glass than listen to another one of Dr. Pei's lectures."

Balanced Centered Marissa: This is a tough one to swallow… especially since glass cuts! This horrific insult came from one of my MBA students when I was lecturing at the Anderson Graduate School of Management at UCLA. It was a big class and I had many, many, positive reviews, but that ugly one really hurt. My Internal Critic Rose will actually pull this one out of her bag of tricks when she's on a roll and it does feel sharp and uncomfortable. It bursts whatever balloon I'm floating up in and the deep dark doubts about who I am surface once again. If I am not vigilant with my Balanced Centered Marissa, my sad one Sarah will take over and we will go down the rabbit hole again to wallow in feelings and BS Belief Systems of unworthiness and worthlessness. So, to head Rose off at the pass, I tell it like it is… "Yes, that was a mean comment, and to be honest, I was a really good lecturer, but I was young. And I did like being the youngest at everything; my competitive part of me that is mostly awesome does get me into turtle soup every once in awhile. And so were all of my lectures fabulous? No. Could I have done better? Of course. Did I do pretty well with the time that I had, the place I was in my life and the resources that I'd been given? Absolutely. I will not have 100% love or approval anywhere I go in life. And it will serve me to be okay with that."

So, the soothing is a muscle, one that takes continuous practice for the Balanced Centered part of me. Now it's your turn to play the Insulting Game.

List the Insults that your Critic keeps playing in your head and then go back and write down what your Balanced Centered Self says to soothe both your Critic and your Brat.

INSULTS:

Critic	BCS

There's another Balance Tool that can help us stretch and improve our Free to Be Me Endurance.

Balance Tool: Bake Your Own Cake

I'm actually known for this expression and it's funny, when I go and give keynotes and I don't put it in the presentation, people will actually come up to me and say they were disappointed that I didn't talk about this concept. So here it is!

In moving from ego-ridden fear to the freedom to be me, it is fundamental to be able to bake your own cake. What I mean by that is if we are constantly looking for approval from others to feel happy, then we are going to be walking unsteadily through life. When we get compliments or recognition or Like's we will feel good about ourselves. On the other hand, if we don't get Likes or acknowledgement or appreciation from others, we will fall like a soufflé, and it will be difficult to get us to rise again. So how do you start baking?

- Step 1: Mix the answers to the following questions in a bowl.

   What am I good at? Remember compliments that people have given you over the years…

   I'll use myself as an example because this is also the balancing out of the last Insult Exercise:

   I love your style.

   You are a genius with words.

   You are such a great communicator.

   You can read my mind.

You are so helpful.

You have a strong voice.

You have a really good eye.

You have a way with people.

You have a way with words.

You are a great writer.

You are a wonderful talk radio host.

The camera loves you.

- Step 2. Fold in the compliments and find the core of who you are

    For the longest time, I could not accept compliments. I would shake my head and say "No, not really." Or, I would be gracious enough to say, "Thank You," but then inside my Critic would go nuts with the same, "Oh, they say that because they don't know you yet." I can remember repeating like a song, "I wish I could see myself half as fabulous as people say I am... then I'd be happy." It's as if I could not shake the voices that kept me on the "Peace of Shiitake" side of the swing. Since I couldn't believe myself, I would constantly be performing and scanning my audience for admirers...waiting and hoping for another compliment so I could temporarily feel good about myself again. I see many of my executive coaching clients slip on these stages. Their audience was not kind, or wrapped up in their own drama, so that acknowledgement and appreciation were few and far between.

- Step 3. Bake in your goodness

    Baking your own cake means that you look at the compliments not as the main ingredient of your life, but just icing. You bake the core cake of who you are, the good bad and the not so good parts of you and validate yourself. So, from that list of compliments, own your cake. You are free to be who you are and that is your foundation cake. No one's words of praise or criticism can bake the cake… it's just icing.

- Step 4. Combine yourself

 So, carrying on with my example, my cake is made up of:

 1/4 cup kindness

 1/8 cup funny

 1/8 cup smart

 1/16 cup generosity

 1/4 cup creativity

 1/16 cup impatience and overly critical

 1/16 cup determination

 1/16 cup resilience

And my cake is solid… it doesn't change with circumstances, when shift happens and there is a missed understanding or missed take or intent doesn't equal impact, or imperfection hits… it doesn't change the core of who I am in my cake. When I get a compliment or a criticism it's all the same… it is just icing on my cake. It may make me taste life a little sweeter, but it doesn't ruin me one way or the other.

 Okay, now it's your turn to bake your own cake!

Step 1: Mix the answers to the following questions in a bowl:

 What am I good at? Remember compliments that people have given you over the years…

_____

_____

_____

_____

_____

_____

_____

_____

Step 2. Fold in the compliments and find the core of who you are. Who are you free to be at your core?

_____

_____

_____

_____

_____

_____

Step 3. Bake in your goodness

_____

_____

_____

_____

_____

_____

Now you are ready to set your cake at 350 degrees in your Oven of Life. Don't forget to take it out and cool down so that you can also enjoy the 'icing' compliments and occasional criticisms that are sure to come!

☯ Balance Tool: Free to Dream

Now that we have chosen not to live in Fear, we can relax, breathe, and dream! Fear keeps us so preoccupied with protecting ourselves and our stuff that we stifle our ability to dream. In fact, Dr. Michael Bernard Beckwith says that most of us suffer from IDD, not ADD or ADHD. Fear keeps us suffering from Intention Deficit Disorder. My favorite line from the movie *Flashdance* is, "When you stop dreaming, you die." So, now that you are moving out of Fear into Freedom, here's an exercise that lets you engage your Freedom to Dream. I borrow this phrase from another one of my influential teachers, Abraham through Esther Hicks. You use the prompter, "Wouldn't it be nice if," and then fill in the blank without evaluating or using the Fear Factor to stunt your dreams. Here's mine:

Wouldn't it be nice if…?

- I have 8 million dollars to be generous with
- To buy an 8 room home on the beach
- With a music room
- And a sewing room
- And an art room
- And a photography room
- And a children's story room
- And a library
- And a gourmet kitchen
- And a walk in closet
- And a rooftop deck
- And a daily housekeeper
- And a driver
- And a radio show
- And a TV show
- And a book publishing company
- And bestselling books
- And a base to find and promote writers of love, in word and song
- And a game show
- And children's shows

- That all promote love joy peace prosperity generosity and creativity
- And a boutique for all original designs inspired by this life
- And the funds to be generous with to others to promote their gifts talents and abilities
- To let them heal
- To help them heal
- To be of service
- And of benefit
- To be essential

And so it is.

Your turn. Fill in the blanks below:

Wouldn't it be nice if…?

_____

_____

_____

_____

_____

_____

_____

_____

_____

_____

_____

_____

_____

_____

_____

_____

Now that you've set your intentions, you can let them go into the care of a Friendly Universe. You don't need to come back and check and impatiently say, "Well, it's not here yet and it's never really going to happen." As Abraham tells us through Esther Hicks, you have launched your rocket of desire and now you just have to go about your inspired business and stay feeling in the most positive place and be a point of positive attraction and good things will begin to happen. At the risk of bragging, I went from a place of fear, hatred, loneliness, shame, loss, heartbreak, perfectionism, and being out of control to attracting incredible people places and things into my life. In these last 8+ years of practicing what I am teaching you here, I have attracted:

- Awards plentiful including the 2017 Iconic Women of the Year, the 2016 Podcast of the Year Top 10 in Health Award, the OC 99 List of Influential Business Leaders, the 2014 Asian Heritage Award, 2014 Lotus Business Person of the Year Award, the 2012 Asian Entrepreneur of the Year Award, the 2007 Remarkable Woman of the Year Award and the 2005 Role Model of the Year Award in Business and Media.
- Network TV interviews and appearances
- A-List guests and Red Carpet interviews
- Enough money to pay off almost all of the $465,000 judgement in the divorce
- Starting over after losing a consulting company valued up to $2 million
- Outstanding feedback from corporate and private coaching clients
- Enough money to raise 2 beautiful girls on my own and one is now at an Ivy league college

- A lecture tour in China
- Peace work trips to teach and speak in Africa, Brazil, Canada, Peru
- An article written about me in the Inc. magazine and in the Hearst fashion magazine Marie Claire China
- Photo Credit and an article about me in Forbes magazine and a regular column in the newspaper
- A new arena of Broadcast Journalism (and my Grade 9 English teacher told me I was a horrible writer)
- and yes, a NY book contract!

And all because I gave myself the same treatment in all 8 of these chapters as I am giving you… and if it can work for me, it can definitely work for you! Try it, I dare you!!

I'll close this chapter with a reminder of the most powerful tool you have in Life… the Freedom that comes with Choice. And the following things are also free… they don't cost you a dime! You and I are

- Free to choose faith or fear
- Free to love
- Free to decide to be free
- Free to breathe
- Free to release anger
- Free to forgive
- Free to give attention
- Free to see
- Free to understand
- Free to help
- Free to be
- Free to dance
- Free to sing
- Free to dream
- Free to vibrate
- Free to smile
- Free to laugh

- Free to make whole
- Free to believe
- Free to release envy
- Free to release resentment
- Free to make peace not war
- Free to create
- Free to design
- Free to be whole and finally,
- Free to Breathe

I hope I've made a sufficient case to move out of Fear into Freedom. You have so much to gain, and it's never too late to step into Freedom… it's your choice!

I am a free soul.

I am completely, positively and eternally free.

I am free from doubt, fear or unhappiness, today and forever.

—Ernest Holmes, *This Thing Called You*

CHAPTER 7

Out of Perfectionism...into Joy

So, the truth is, I'm a recovering perfectionist. I have spent my lifetime trying to be perfect and when I fall short, I just try to look perfect... can you can relate?

CHECK ALL THAT APPLY

- ❑ I like looking good
- ❑ I want everything to be perfect
- ❑ I love the expression, getting my 'ducks in a row'
- ❑ I love compliments
- ❑ When I get 99 compliments and one insult, I ruminate on that one ugly thought
- ❑ When people screw up I get very irritated
- ❑ I don't understand what the big deal is...it's not rocket science!
- ❑ I've been told I am hard on people
- ❑ I don't ask for anymore from people than I ask from myself
- ❑ I expect a lot from others because it's good for them
- ❑ I expect more from myself than I do anyone else
- ❑ I am harder on myself than I am on anyone else
- ❑ I like being known as a hard worker
- ❑ I like being known for my high standards even though some people call me names that sound like a female dog
- ❑ You say perfectionist like it's a bad thing!

Sound Familiar?

Chloe: It's a good thing being a perfectionist, right? I mean, it gets me on the fast track and people like hard workers. I want to get ahead. I want to have a good reputation. I want that promotion. I want to be seen as the cream of the crop... even though sometimes I taste sour. I want faster... what's wrong with that?

Let Me Give You A "Peace" of My Mind

There's only one thing wrong with perfectionism... nothing and no one is ever enough... including myself.

- I'll relax when this project is over.
- Ok I lied, I'll be happy when I hit my year end goals.
- I'll be happy when I have $50,000 saved in the bank.
- I'll feel better when I make $100,000 a year, well maybe $200,000, no a million, well that doesn't buy anything anymore...a billion?
- I'll be happy when I finish this degree.
- I'll be happy when I get this job, no that job, no that promotion, no that position....
- I'll be happy when my kids start school, finish school, get into a good college, finish college, get a good job, get a better job...
- I'll be happy when my mom gets through this cancer thing, my thing, my kid's thing, my friend's thing...

Sound Familiar?

And then you die.

And you were only happy for the briefest of moments before your perfectionism stole your smile away.

Foundation Peace: The Dis-Ease of Perfectionism

So, what's the downside of being a perfectionist? Let me illustrate with my 88% Model...sorry my inner professor is coming out of retirement!

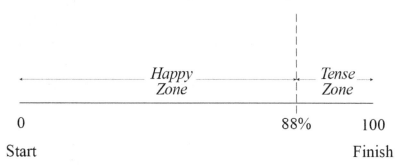

Perfectionists are go-getters. We are given a goal and we are off, we zoom quickly and efficiently with discipline and hard work all the way to the 88% mark. And perfectionists are the usually the first to reach the furthest mark by the end of the day. On the right side of the line is the 12% still not done, still to do, still unfinished, on the "To Do" List that has to get carried over to tomorrow. The good news is we have accomplished most of the task... 88% is a lot of good work done! But we don't stand at that almost done mark to marvel at how much has been done, how much has already been completed, how well we did... the appreciation side of the line. No that's a waste of time because we're not finished. We can pat ourselves on the back only when we are 100% done!

So, we almost always stand on that 88% point and face the 100% Finish Line. The good news about that 12% gap is that it gives us the motivation and the forward motion to get to 100%. The bad news is two-fold. First, it's not a very pleasant place to be. It feels incomplete and therefore not satisfying. It sings the "What's wrong? What's not done? What's still not complete?" song. We won't be happy until we cross that Finish line. Second, we rarely get to the 100% mark! Yes, we finish the task, the goal, the mission but it's a passing fly-by acknowledgement, a drive-by 'good job' hurled at our staff or team members or family members and we are off to complete the next task, goal or mission. We rarely acknowledge the completion to ourselves and worse off, we forget to be grateful to those who have helped us along the way. Yes, perfectionists are not the easiest to people to work with!

To make matters worse, perfectionists treat people the same way. I use the analogy with my dates, since my perfectionism keeps my relationships short of the term boyfriend! When I do have time to date, I don't date Mr. Loser, who is at the 0% mark on the line. I also can't find Mr. Perfect, who would be at the 100% end of the line. I usually end up with Mr. 88%, who is mostly great. However, just like I do in my professional life, I also stand at that 88% line and face the 100% asking why my guy does all of the things that make me crazy! If he liked/loved me, he would stop leaving the seat up, or toothpaste mangled, or text back faster, or show up on time, or, or, or… and focusing on that 12% absolutely gives me that same uneasy uncomfortable tense unfinished feeling… definitely not happy! If I turned around and faced the Start line and focused instead on the 88% I would see all the wonderful things he does do and say and is… and I would definitely have more smiles in that direction!

This model helps perfectionists understand their Dis-ease and how it can be treated with appreciation instead of criticism. Asking "what's right with me, it, him, her, they, the situation" will definitely increase your joy and happiness factor to 88%. Conversely, asking "what's wrong with him, her, them, the world, me?" usually leads to throw up our hands and saying that the world is going to heck in a handbasket!

I remember reading in *Fortune* magazine some years back that the two biggest barriers to leadership success were perfectionism and taking things too personally. Working with my executive coaching clients, successful top three levels of leadership in Fortune 100 companies, and private life Balance coaching clients who followed the same high achieving path, I would definitely concur! And, if you haven't figured it out, I'm preaching to the choir. But I am now a recovering perfectionist 88% of the time, so you're in good hands! If you have been on the "fast track" and now you are feeling derailed then read on.

Let Me Give You A "Peace" of My Mind

Perfectionism seems to work for many people for a few decades. You can see the tell-tale signs: super achievement oriented, busy, really busy, multi-talented, opinionated, constantly giving advice, constantly being asked for advice, is an expert in at least 2 things, burning a candle, or candelabra at all ends, multiple balls in the air, possibly ADD or ADHD but not in the right generation to have been diagnosed, going, going, and gone!

Usually around mid-life crisis time, which I've renamed to mid-life opportunity, there is a breakdown. Sometimes it follows what I call the Perfectionist Slide…Perfectionism, Procrastination and then Paralysis. We want to do everything perfectly… and when we don't think the conditions are right, we procrastinate. Aside, I've always wanted to be a procrastinator but I never got around to it, ha! Sorry, that is one of my favorite quips from Steven Wright. And then when the consequences of procrastination catches up with us, we end up in Paralysis… so far behind that we stop answering phones, opening mail, caring at all.

So how do we get trapped into this box called Perfectionism? Let's take a look at each of the sides that keep us trapped in a limited space of happiness. Are you ready to open up?

Foundation Peace: Perfection and Validation

Perfectionism Box Side 1:

If I am perfect, I will get the love that I didn't get growing up.

Many of us grow up being criticized over and over and over and over again. Nothing we say or do is ever enough good enough or perfect enough.

> *Maria*: I tried so hard to please my mom. I remember as a child being in the kitchen after dinner… I think I was 7 or 8 years of age, and I cleared the table, washed the dishes, wiped

down the stove, put the leftovers away in the fridge, swept the floor and cleaned the countertops… all by myself. I rushed upstairs to ask my mom to come down and say the words I would spend a lifetime yearning to hear "Wow, that's wonderful Maria…I'm so proud of you!" She came down the stairs, inspected the kitchen and said, "You didn't push in the chairs," then turned around and walked back up the stairs.

Like Maria, many of us carry that desire to please from childhood into adulthood like a bad habit. Then, throughout our lifetime, we attract people who are difficult to please over and over again. Many of my clients move from an un-pleasable parent to an un-pleasable spouse to an un-pleasable boss and so on, always hoping to hear those magic words, "You're beautiful, you're precious, you matter, you are enough," and not receiving them. So, perfectionism becomes a default habit, and we may or may not be conscious of it, but the underlying desire is to get it right so that we can finally be given the love that was never there for us. If this sounds like you, you might want to try the following Balance Tool.

Learning in Action with Balance Tools

☯ Balance Tool: Don't Go to the Tractor for Milk!

Take a breath. Think about all of the people in your life who you stand on your head for, and it still isn't enough. A friend, a boss, a coworker, a family member, a partner, a wasband, an insignificant other…anyone who is INCAPABLE of being responsive, respectful, caring, gracious no matter how kind, responsive, caring, respectful and gracious you are. People who you stay up at night writing a perfect letter to, hoping that when they read it, they will finally understand you and change. You know who I am talking about… we all have at least one tractor in our lives! The good news is we attracted them to try to resolve the unfulfilled love in our past and the bad news is we will keep attracting them until we can stop trying to get milk from a tractor and find the cow that is actually us!!

Take a minute now to stop and take the Tractor Oath:

I, _____ (your Balanced Centered Self name) promise from this moment forward to stop looking to _____ (the name(s) of your tractors) for appreciation, recognition, approval, encouragement, understanding and validation which for whatever reason, they are not able to give me. I take responsibility for attracting them into my life to resolve unloved issues from the past or because I like feeling unfulfilled and in drama. I will use the Balance Tool from Chapter 6 to Bake my own cake so I can give myself the approval that I've been hoping for. I am a beautiful cow with a limitless supply of milk. And so it is!

Foundation Peace: Perfection and Self-Acceptance

Perfectionism Box Side 2: I hate the ugly parts of myself. I'm really not OK.

As I mentioned in the last chapter, I used to say to myself, I wish I could feel half as good about myself as people think I am. And no matter how many compliments I would get, I knew that if they really got to know me, they would realize I'm really not that great and leave. It's just a matter of time before I get found out. So, I spend exorbitant amounts of energy hiding that insecurity with perfectionism. All that matters is that I look good on the outside and hide the insecurity on the inside. We end up feeling like an imposter in our own body, feeling like an actor on life's stage, pretending to be who we are. Relationships get tricky because we are afraid to show our true selves in case we are "found out" so we only let people so close. Sound familiar?

Where do we get the message that we are not okay? In my case it obviously started from my mother, but she is not to blame for all of it. I used to think that only abused kids had this self-hatred. But as I relayed to you in the last chapter, I discovered after doing hundreds of career day presentations that around the age of 10, even healthy kids somehow develop the lie that they are not good enough, that they are not thin enough, not smart enough, not worthy, not pretty, not ok as they are. And this seed, if planted in the right life dirt, fertilized by parents teachers and peers reinforcing that lie, will grow into a giant weed that chokes out the Light of Love for oneself. The good news is that you can actually replace that seed with new ones like the message I got from my Grade 10 math teacher. Because of the constant negative mantras I received at home, I worked really hard to prove myself. I don't know if it was the haunting look in my eyes, my perfectionism or the slump of my shoulders that led to my teacher asking me to stay after class one day. He sat down on his desk and looked straight into my eyes and said "Maria, you will achieve anything you want in life if you put your heart and mind into it". Those words gave me the hope that has lasted me a lifetime. And because of JJ Bristow, I make a point at every career day presentation to give the same monumental message to kids that was given to me. And if you caught the name change in the example, I actually changed my name from Maria to Marissa after high school when I modeled full-time. I wanted to leave "UGLY" Maria behind, so I became Marissa. So, treating perfectionism starts with letting go of the lies that there's something wrong with us.

Foundation Peace: The Binding Myth of Perfection

Perfectionism Box Side 3: But I really can be perfect and I will keep trying to perfect even if it kills me…and if you find fault with me or in me, beware! And I will do everything to make sure that I look perfect on the outside!! And so, perfectionists have a VERY DIFFICULT TIME taking criticism…sound familiar? I love the expression, "Yes, please give me feedback… but can you try to not get it all over me?" I can never sit still long enough in a learning forum to focus on any of the compliments when I am being evaluated… I just zoom straight to the "criticism" and then beat myself up for failing once again in not being perfect. I can remember being asked by internship boss, "Do you really want to be perfect?" And my answer was a fast YES! And there was and still is a tiny part of me that really believes that I am close and eventually can be. Relate?

Don't be afraid to admit it… that's why I say 88% all of the time! Until I let go of that fantasy, that need, that angst that I can and will be perfect, I will have the disease that will keep me on that hamster wheel trying desperately to be perfect and killing myself in the effort.

So here are some Balance Tools to help see ourselves as perfectly imperfect and accepting that that is okay…so that our perfectionism doesn't drive our life car off a cliff.

☯ Balance Tool: Detonate the Hot Button with The Imperfect Exercise

I used to hate it when my family would say to me "You're *SO SENSI-TIVE*". And so, I refused to show any feeling or tears or compassion… I threw out the baby with the bath water. Because I hated that part of myself, I reacted, and then I overcompensated in the other direction. When people used to say, "Who do you think you are?" Or "You are such a self-promoter," I would feel myself getting defensive and angry with a loud "How Dare You!!" Hot buttons are aggravating… we hate when they're pushed. However, they can be a valuable indicator light that tells us where we have an opportunity to heal. If there are insults that are still stuck in your emotional craw, it's time to defuse.

Because we are not perfect. We do have a few qualities that are not fabulous. When we can own them, the button becomes less atomic.

- I am impatient.
- I am critical and judgmental.
- I am selfish.
- I am a self-promoter.
- I can be overly sensitive.

These are parts of myself that I don't like and are my hot buttons. Because I don't like them, I don't want you to see them either and when you do, I become an egomaniac with an inferiority complex, and explode. Once I am honest and aware of my hot buttons, I can detonate by balancing them out with my assets.

I am also caring, loving, smart, funny, witty, creative, communicative, friendly, astute, fashionable, musical, organized, disciplined, positive, expressive, and artistic.

Another way to detonate your hot button is to recognize that even the negative traits have an upside.

Research is showing a direct correlation between sensitivity and creativity.

Because I am critical I am also a good discerner and problem solver.

Because I am selfish, I see opportunities to have my needs met. And I am not always selfish. And there's a healthy part of being selfish that's called self-care.

I have no fear to step up to the plate to self-promote, which is actually marketing and sales, which is an important part of my business. I am just being my own publicist… and that saves money!

So now your turn to practice.

Take a breath.

Now list all of those negative things that you've been criticized for. It might be similar to the Insulting Exercise we did in the last chapter, but this time focus on all of those areas that you do know deep, deep down are true about you and you are not happy with… those things that you wish you weren't and list them:

I WISH I WASN'T SO…

_____   _____

_____   _____

_____   _____

_____   _____

_____   _____

_____   _____

_____   _____
_____   _____

Okay, back to the Voices in Our Head.

Your Critic has had a field day with all of these on the list.

Now it's your Balanced Centered Self's turn to respond and soothe.

First list those positive things that you are as well.

I AM…

_____

_____

_____

_____

_____

_____

_____

_____

Now go back to each of the negative ones and list next to them in the adjacent column the upside of those qualities.

Whenever your Critic starts hammering you on your imperfect qualities, you can come back to this exercise and point out to he/her that we've already covered our downside and it's time to balance it out with our upside and the upside of our downside.

Defusing is a skill. The ability to hear a criticism and not run or shrink or turtle or spit back is a skill. The ability to refrain from saying in retaliation, "If I looked like you I'd be miserable too!" or "I wouldn't want to be you!" is a skill.

Strengthen your Balanced Centered Self to say, "I am 88% Perfect" and that's Perfect. I am imperfectly perfect exactly as I am. I can be okay with the 12% ugly part of me. I can embrace even those parts of me that get triggered by other people's criticism and insults. It's not easy but it will certainly shift me into the 88% happy place. Once I have owned my side of the street I can let go of my hot button quickly and get by into my Joy spot. Another way to address people's poking at us is the next Balance tool, which I've coined "Finding the polish in the rub".

☯ Balance Tool: Find the Polish in the Rub

When people rub you the wrong way, insult you, talk about you behind your back, talk smack to you in front of your back, perfectionists can have a few habitual extreme reactions. One, they are indignant, and our internal Brat says, "How dare you! I have been nothing but nice to you! Screw you; I am taking my toys and going home!" The Sad One turns inside and is mortified. All of the fears of being found out as not as great as you are trying to look lands on you like bird poop. The Sad One bows her head and wants to cry. Then the Brat or Critic wants to come back and fight and defend and explain why the insult was not true. In the prior Imperfect exercise, we learned how to be okay with the good bad and ugly part of the perfectionist. In this exercise, we take the rub and find the polish… what is this irritation from others helping me develop?

Recently I heard that my name was being pulled through the mud on a planning conference call that I wasn't able to make. My initial Agnes the Brat reaction was human… I wanted to take my toys and go home. I wouldn't help with the event at all. I couldn't believe that a person who I thought liked admired and respected me brought up past dirt that I didn't even know was on her mind! I really wanted to go on the attack and spew, "I heard you bash me in a group call behind my back about something that happened so long ago that you didn't bother telling me about at all and now you are spreading shitake about me to people that I don't even know and bad-mouthing my character?! How dare you? And worse yet, I thought we had a great loving relationship… I will definitely give you a wide berth and minimize any future interactions with you. I will definitely let everyone know the kind of person you are. And to think I've been taking your side when rumors have been running rampant about you!" Then Rose my Critic turned on me… "Now you really know how people feel about you. They think you're going to take over the event, that you are going to self-promote, that it's not going to be about anyone but you and that's because you are selfish self-centered narcissistic and horrible just like you know you are!!" And in the past, that's when I would either run or fight and defend and say… take a guess! Now that I'm writing this book, and trying to practice what I preach, I have a different formula to move myself from trying to prove that I am perfect to myself and others, to choosing steps that will bring me back into Joy. By taking a purifying look at the rubbing irritating interaction, I can grow from the experience and polish myself.

Now it's your turn. Is there a negative interaction from your past that keeps playing in your uneasy head like a broken record? Take a moment now and see if you can't find the polish in the rub:

Describe what happened:

_____

_____

_____

_____

_____

_____

_____

_____

Now what is your reaction from your Brat, your Sad One and your Critic?

My Brat says:

_____

_____

_____

_____

My Sad One says:

_____

_____

_____

_____

My Critic says:

_____

_____

_____

_____

What can your Balanced Centered Self say to soothe you and come out of the perfectionistic retaliation reaction back into Joy? I use another Balance Tool called the Serenity Prayer to help me find the polish in the rub and now you can too.

Balance Tool: The Serenity Prayer

God, Grant me the Serenity…because that's what I want

To Accept the Things I Cannot Change… like what people think of me, that my positive aspects of me like strength and no fear and 'out there' and big voice and good marketer and communications queen are not always going to hit at the right time and sometimes will hit a nerve…

The Courage to Change the Things I can…like maybe I can pause before saying and acting to see if the timing is best, that I may need to care less what people think when I am out to change the world, that I can find the polish in the rub and then cut people the same slack that I would like to have given to me, that I wouldn't want to trade in my strong personality that helps me to be a Beneficial Presence on the Planet most of the time because once in a while I step in it…

And the Wisdom to know the Difference… when to Hold and when to Fold.

Amen.

Now it's your turn…

God, Grant me the Serenity… because that's what I want

To Accept the Things I Cannot Change…like what people think of me, that I my positive aspects of me like…

_____

_____

_____

_____

The Courage to Change the Things I can… like maybe I can

_____

_____

_____

_____

And the Wisdom to know the Difference… when to Hold and when to Fold.

Amen.

Now let's turn back to address the 4th and last side of our Perfectionism Box that keeps us isolated from Joy.

Foundation Peace: You Have to be Perfect, too

Perfectionism Box Side #4:

Perfectionism is a disease or Dis-Ease that not only robs ourselves of joy, it also makes us miserable to be around because we can suck the joy out of our friends, family, coworkers, partners and more. Not only do we expect ourselves to be perfect, we expect people around us to be perfect too!!

I have been told more than once that I am hard on people… that I have unrealistic expectations that normal people can't possibly live up to. I keep insisting that I don't, but my lack of close friends is a telltale sign that there may be some truth in that feedback.

If I want people to like, love and accept me the way I am, 88% perfect, then I really have to do the same with others. I get what I give… so giving others a break gets me that same break.

I can hear some of you objecting at this point about the feasibility of 88%. As an organizational psychologist, I get to work with many high-achieving perfectionists who try to negotiate with me on my 88% perfect rule… my finance clients especially. "We can't afford to have a 12% error margin!" True, in budgeting and science and accounting and flying airplanes, the 88% is probably not a good idea. But when it comes to how we see ourselves and others, the principle of cutting people a little bit of slack will go a long way to lessen perfectionistic anxiety and increase our joy factor.

To practice being okay with imperfection with myself and others, I challenge myself with a few fun exercises:

With myself:

- I put my underwear on inside out.
- When I get a tiny smudge on my manicure, I don't redo it.
- I wear two different colored socks.
- I don't redo eyeliner that is not perfect.

With others:

- When I catch a mistake that is not that big of a deal I don't point it out.
- I don't autocorrect others.
- I ask myself before I speak, "Is it true? Is it kind? Is it necessary?" and if I can't get all three of them right, I keep my mouth shut. I learned that fabulous happiness heuristic from the late Dr. David Simon when I heard him speak at his celebration of life ceremony at the Chopra Center in La Jolla before he transitioned. The world would be an amazing place if everyone adopted this rule.

☯ Balance Tool: Vent Partner

Another common characteristic perfectionists share is a zero-to-100 road to frustration, exasperation and irritation… because of the impossible standards we hold for ourselves and others. Vent partnering is a tool that helps the Perfectionist release that negative energy which by the way takes up more volume/room than positive energy, back into the air and out of the body and mind. If we don't release that negative energy, it will get trapped and infected into resentment and anger which means you'll have to go back and read Chapter 4 all over again! So, try this practice… it's a favorite with my corporate clients.

Pick someone who you don't like… just kidding… someone who you trust to be your vent partner (VP). Every day you are allowed two minutes to spend with your VP venting and releasing your frustrations. Here are some rules to follow:

1. Spend equal amounts of time listening and venting. When venting, limit the spew to two minutes once, or maximum, twice a day. And then allow them to return the favor.

2. The listener is not allowed to problem solve or give advice, nor try to top the vent with "Oh if you think that's bad, listen to what he did to me…" but commiserating comments are allowed: "Oh, I'm so sorry; that must suck".

3. Allow yourself to tell the truth…be honest and ok with not being perfect in your reactions and being triggered. It is important to release the frustration. Medical studies are clear now that internalized stress will impact your health. That one is a hard one for me, I want to be able to always react with love. That perfect non-vulnerable veneer doesn't engender me to many people because people don't like people who are perfect, or pretend to be perfect. I am still and will probably always struggle with this one.

4. Swearing is allowed if both are okay with it.

5. If you do not use your two minutes, you do not get to 'roll them over' like Cingular to the next day… so take advantage of the time.

6. If you don't feel safe with anyone, use your computer as your vent partner and write an email to yourself… and then hit Save Draft. I used to say to write the vent to the offender and hit Save Draft, but I had too many clients accidentally hit SEND, so we adjusted the To: to Self. If you just want to let off steam without writing, stomping up and down the stairwell or fast jogging with the offender's face on the step or asphalt is a good vent as well. I used to also advise going to your car in the parking garage, rolling up the windows and screaming for 10-18 seconds, but as a singer, I know it hurts your voice, so now I recommend silent screaming which contorts your face but not your lungs.

7. The vent is like Vegas… what is said in Vegas stays in Vegas, so the agreement for confidentiality is very important. The damage from "Now don't tell anyone… but you should have heard what _____ said about _____!" ruins the exercise and possibly will end your career if you are venting about your boss!

8. Once the vent is complete, YOU ARE NOT ALLOWED TO GO OVER IT AGAIN. Obviously from my Caps, this is a tough one. But there is a very good reason why I *insist on this rule. It's called the Law of Attraction.*

Foundation Peace: The Law of Attraction

If you think I'm about to launch into a lesson on how to attract money, cars and a hot body into your life, I'm not. That's actually the Law of Intention, which I may address in my next book, *8 Ways to Pleasure*! But I am going to share how this spiritual law, as it has been taught to me by one of my important life teachers Abraham through Esther and Jerry Hicks, because it has been immensely helpful in choosing my own joy and happiness 88% of the time. And it is a simple and as difficult as this… whatever we focus on for sixteen seconds attracts a like thought and/or feeling to match it. So, it works to make you feel better AND to feel worse. So that's why once you have vented about a certain person place or thing, that's it…it's over and out. Because if you keep it alive by talking about it over and over again, or thinking about it incessantly, or being mad or sad about it all the time, it will grow… and quickly.

The good news is if you are having a good heartwarming, mind-lightening thought about a certain person place or thing, then another thought like it that is heartwarming and mind lightening will join it…and since thoughts turn into things, you will attract positive or negative people places and situations depending on what you are paying attention to and talking about. For the past three years I have been practicing this Law stringently. Anytime a negative thought or circumstance crosses my mental emotional or physical path, I feel it fully in less than 16 seconds, release it, and then turn my attention to something that makes me feel better.

I don't make stuff up about how that person will miraculously change or that a million dollars will rain on my parade, but I do pivot as quickly as possible to a better feeling thought, which is usually as quickly as remembering positive interactions with people places things and situations, which then lead to new positive interactions and so on and so on so that the next thing I know I am doing the Abun-Dance again! OK, time to practice.

 ## Balance Tool: Turning on a Dime of Memories

Take a breath.…

Now identify things in your life that make you feel good inside. Store these memories in your heart to pull out anytime you're ready to pivot and make shift happen when shiitake happens.

I love remembering

- Having my daughters' friends complement them on clothes and shoes that they took from my closet
- Being told that their friends wish that I was their mom rather than their own
- Being told by your daughter that she's glad that I'm not an uptight mom like her friends' moms
- For being appreciated when I volunteer at her school
- For the 15 years I taught all of their friends how to say "Happy Chinese New Year" in Mandarin
- Have their friends' faces light up when they got a dollar bill in their Chinese New Year Red packet
- Have my daughters' faces light up when I buy something that they like
- The sound of my daughters laughing together when they're talking with each other
- The sound of my daughter's' laughter when she's laughing at something that I am joking about
- When they show me things that are hip and cool and I get to join in their laughter
- Reading new menus of items I've never tried before at a restaurant that's been recommended
- For the ease of writing with Siri
- When Siri tells me that "It's a good thing you canceled that meeting because you're too busy anyway!"
- When voice recognition makes up something funny and stupid from what I tried to say
- Finding a great shoe deal
- Falling in love with a dress or shoe on a bargain rack and having it look fabulous on me

- Having your friend tell you that if you hear a noise in the middle of the night it will be her breaking into my closet
- Being thanked for helping people, for making a positive difference in their life
- Free-flowing traffic on your side of the freeway while it's bumper-to-bumper on the other side… Borderline (but I'm not perfect ha ha)
- Freshly washed car and full tank of gas
- Listening to your daughter sing in the shower
- Listening to your daughter teach herself how to play the guitar
- Finding the perfect parking spot
- Step on the scale and seeing the number drop
- Keeping commitments to myself, especially when it comes to weight loss
- Watching dogs play at the dog park and at the dog beach
- Seeing a dog with its head out of the window enjoying the wind
- Knowing I'm going to see a dolphin and seeing one
- Having a dolphin jump up in the air in front of me on the anniversary of my father's transition
- Watching babies play with each other
- Remembering when my daughters would laugh at nothing and everything
- Feeling myself tear up with joy because I love my life and I love being woken up early to write even though I protest at first
- For the feeling of coming up or really allowing a brilliant saying, teaching, concept, idea in a creative moment which comes often
- Waking up to the sound of birds singing for no reason at all outside my window
- For the delight of anticipation of a fun weekend, week, month, year, trip, weekend away, work, play
- For realizing that I have lost the distinction between work and play
- For the feeling of my scrumptious bed

And I have just completed what Esther and Abraham call a Rampage of Appreciation. I have primed my life pump away from the Box of Perfectionism and into the infinity pool of Joy and Possibilities. Now it's your turn… take a breath. Write down memories of people places and things that make you smile.

THINGS THAT I LOVE TO REMEMBER:

_____

_____

_____

_____

_____

_____

_____

_____

_____

_____

_____

_____

☯ Balance Tool: Choose to Soothe with a Better Feeling Thought

Now we can use these good memories and pull them out of your life pocket anytime you want to pivot out of where you are…especially when you are tempted to go down that rabbit hole of a shiitake feeling.

What's the best feeling thought to choose when you find yourself in the dis-ease of perfectionism or loneliness or hatred or loss or shame or fear? This question also comes out of my training with Abraham and Esther Hicks. When we are triggered and are sliding down that slippery slope which will eliminate happiness from your path, there is a strong temptation to make blanket statements or jump into judgment or think that NOTHING WILL EVER CHANGE!! And unfortunately according to the Law of Attraction, that will be your experience. One of the psychological phenomena the Pygmalion Effect that I introduced earlier in the Dating Pump section also applies to this situation… it's the opposite of "I'll believe it when I see it"… it's actually "I see it because I believe it"! Our BS Belief System filters what we actually pay attention to and when we are locked in trying to control others, we also only see where they are missing the boat because we are locked into our habitual thoughts about them. We can't see when they are actually doing well because of the Pygmalion Effect. Then, another similar psychological effect takes over called Groupthink… when groups of people now cannot see any data that disagrees with their point of view. To help you avoid going down this path to unhappiness try the following soothing Balanced Centered Self statements which you are getting better at using with practice in every chapter:

- It won't always feel like this…
- If things aren't going right, go left!
- It's going to be okay in the end, and if it's not okay, then it's not the end.
- When you're going through hell, keep going
- A year knows what a day doesn't…
- More will be Revealed.
- Everything happens for our Divine and Best Good.
- Fill in any other sayings that help you stay in a good place

We can reset into Joy and land in a better feeling place when we choose better feeling thoughts. Take a look at this next Balance tool to see if you can help yourself by being aware of where you are before you slip down into perfectionistic criticism of yourself and others.

Balance Tool: Staying out of the Labyrinth of Shiitake

I watch myself and my clients unknowingly slip into and get lost in this thinking pattern that I affectionately call the Labyrinth of Shiitake. We start at the opening with Stinking Thinking, and if we don't catch it early with a better feeling thought it attracts more negative thoughts until the momentum brings us to Worst Case Scenario. If it's a pain somewhere in our body, we suddenly think it's a terminal disease. If we lose something, someone must have stolen it. When the news is tragic, the world is going to Hades in a handbasket. If we continue down the path of worst case scenario far enough, we end up lost in the Effinator, which is everything bad is because I am bad, worthless, unworthy and messed up. Every bad thing that I was told about myself is really true... my mother/father was right, I'll never amount to anything... this is proof. We end up just giving up, staying in bed with the covers over our head, or drowning our thoughts with food, drugs or drink. But there is hope... using this same tool of choosing a better thought, we can work our way back into Joy and Happiness.

Stinkin' Thinkin': "It's gloomy outside. I don't feel like going to work. I have so many meetings today. I hate my job. I'm trapped."

If you can catch yourself here, you might be able to stop the downward trajectory with Balanced Centered Self statements like: "Yes, I am solar-powered. I'm glad this is just June gloom and that the sun will be out soon. I am glad that I live here and not in places where it's gloomy most of the time. I do like a lot of things about work most of the time. It's okay to be in my 12% for a minute...or 16 seconds...take a breath and get out of bed...I wonder what great outfit I'm going to get to put on in my abundant fabulous closet." And boom, I am back in business.

If I don't catch myself and continue with stinkin' thinkin' I move down into Worst Case Scenario: "I want to quit my job but I can't afford it. I am not appreciated there, I deserve a raise, I hate my boss, my coworkers suck and I will be suffering there until retirement, unless of course the administration screws up my pension fund like the company I heard about in the news. Nothing is safe anymore. I will probably end up homeless because

I'll get laid off or the company will go bankrupt and I'll be unemployable because I will be too old to be competitive in the workplace."

If you can catch yourself here, you will have to work a little harder to pivot. You may have to kick yourself up with a big laugh at yourself "God, do I sound pathetically ridiculous or what?!" Have I ever gone without a meal or have a roof over my head? NO. I'm just having one of my 12 % off days and "This Too Shall Pass".

If you don't soothe at this juncture, you may end up completely lost in the Labyrinth of Shiitake… at the Effinator, which is the point at which everything is your fault… you stop blaming others and come to the sad conclusion that you are truly pathetic and that everyone who put you down was right: "My dad was right, I am good for nothing. I should have known, done or said better. I should have worked harder in high school. I should have said leave me alone to the violator. I should have left him a long time ago. I should have known my past would catch up to me. I can't fool myself anymore, I am worthless, unworthy, unloved unloving and unlovable. I give up. Life is not worth living and no one will even know I'm gone." The "woulda-shoulda-coulda" song plays like a broken record and I 'should" on myself incessantly.

At the risk of criticizing the giant pharmaceutical industry, I have many clients that go directly to the Effinator as a side effect from taking anti-anxiety and antidepressants. Suicidal thoughts where there was no history of them is disturbing. But the good news is that you can even find your way out of the Labyrinth of Shiitake when you are lost at the end of the path. You can turn around. You just have to find one better feeling thought. Just one that will then begin the momentum upwards. Try this example on for size.

> "Yes, I feel like shiitake right now. Yes, I feel hopeless. But I won't always feel this way. I know I can feel better eventually. I can't be that ugly, unlovable, or worthless. I have had at least one moment of goodness in this thing called life, haven't I? Let me close my eyes and breathe. What was the last good thing that

happened to me? Nothing. Now, now Brat, that's not true… remember that little 6-year girl that came up to you and complimented your shoes? Remember how you laughed at that? Oh yeah, but that's so superficial, says the Critic. Yes, but doesn't it feel better to remember that? Yes, but you haven't accomplished anything really significant in your life. Thank you, Critic, for your opinion, but that's not true. We have done amazing things big and small and will continue to do so as long as we are breathing, I promise. We just have to stand up in Hope right now… it will get better, ICBW, It Could Be Worse, we could have no soft comfy bed, no food in our fridge, no car in the garage, no job, no arms and no legs… okay, okay Balanced Centered Self, you're right, you can stop being so positive… I'll get up and brush my teeth and start my day over again."

Let Me Give You A "Peace" of My Heart

So, there you have a complete Box of Perfectionism, with four sides that keep you boxed in and seemingly alone. Let's talk about how perfectionism keeps us from having fulfilling relationships with people… how it puts a lid on that box!

Mia is an attractive sociable fun-loving woman. She is adored by many. She is a good person. And she is alone. When she is in a good place, she finds an easy peace inside and outside, knowing that choosing solitaire is a long run better than sitting at a bar, finding solace in the mystique and false toasts of a stranger, or fellow loner, pretending to like being alone. When she is not in a good place, she wonders if she is only fooling herself, that alone is a choice to punish herself.

Many perfectionists have talked themselves into isolation. Do I really really want to be an island? What is the motive behind the motive for wanting to be alone? Am I choosing a life of solitude consciously or unconsciously? Does it serve me well? Relationships can be tricky for perfectionists, so let's put the "moose on the table" again. Have we boxed ourselves into a solitary life because we are afraid to let people in? Are we afraid that if people really knew who we were they would leave us? I know that I let people get so close with a beckoning hand and a big smile… but at a certain distance the other hand becomes a STOP sign.

> *Rebecca*: "I prefer to be alone than with people who are gossipy, or angry, or whiny or boring, or radical, or political, or religious, or weird. And there are plenty of folks who fall into one or more of those categories that want to be friends with me, but I would rather be alone than suffer their company. So, one more night of sneaking into a movie alone is on the menu. Is there an alternative to banishing myself to myself?"

> *Danny*: "Everyone else has plans and no one bothers to ask me. And when I invite others to join me, they always have other plans, or they flake out at the last minute, or don't have time until next week, or next month, or next year. Screw it. I am going to live happily alone on that desert island. Yeah, right. Another version of "I'll just take my toys and go home.""

I have to admit when my friend Julie talks about her high school or elementary friends that she is still going on trips or girlfriend spa days or reunions with on a monthly basis, I feel like a failure…and lonely. Or, when I see girlfriends emulate the *Sex and the City* girls, the same greenish tinge passes over my face. My own track record with best friends is dismal at best.

I actually had a horrible experience that keeps playing in my head like a scratched 45 vinyl record. A girl that I had befriended during college told me that I wasn't her best friend, just a friend, and to not introduce her as such anymore. I was crushed.

Today I understand that I do treat girlfriends the same as boyfriends… I free fall into them and get emotionally involved much like a starfish gets pounded by a tidal wave. A good friend suggested recently that I might want to try "titrating" myself… that not "everything all at once" might work better than the concentrated version of me. I am still rolling that one around in my mouth.

One of my mentors, Mary, suggested that I make a list of the qualities I would like to have in a best friend.

- Someone who I can check in with every day.
- Who is interested in me. Yes, it's still all about me.
- Someone who is my biggest fan.
- Someone who lets me vent.
- Someone who gently nudges me when I am not keeping my side of the street clean after I have already vented.
- Someone I can make plans with on a weekly basis.
- Someone who believes in God the way I do.
- Who is a positive person.
- Who likes to laugh.
- Who likes to watch a good movie.
- Who enjoys great food.
- Who loves her/his work.
- Who feels safe enough to cry on my shoulder. Ok, it's about them too…progress.
- Who keeps my confidences.
- Who says, "sorry."
- Who says, "That sucks a lollipop."

Important question… can I be that friend first?

After I completed the list, I happily realized that I actually had all of those items but not housed in one person. I have 3 women who fulfill all of the items on my list. I was so busy feeling sorry for myself and whining that I didn't have a BFF like my other friends had that I couldn't see the wealth in front of me. Once I released that lie--that you HAD to have one BFF in one person, I got my joy back.

When I take an 88 thousand feet view from above, I have many connections and imperfectly perfect people in my life who love me as I am, who are imperfectly perfect themselves. I have a mentor who has held my hand over the last 21 years, who has loved me through good times and bad. And a sponsor who I check in with every morning for the past 8.8 years. I have a circle of women and men who, like waves, touch me and nourish me one tide at a time. I am not alone. And I am not lonely, 88% of the time!

And the proverbial adage, "be the friend you want to have", works. It is another Law of Attraction at work. If you don't like the people in your life, take a good look at yourself because what you are is attracting… like and like. Once I started being a person that I would like to have as a friend, I began to attract good friends. There is an art and science behind having good friends.

So, have I convinced you to jump out of the box of perfectionism? I still feel some hesitation so the last chapter is for anyone who still feels that life could be so much happier if people would just do what we asked them to do. In other words, "You say 'Control Freak' like it's a bad thing!" So, we move into the last chapter called Out of Control… into Happiness. Recovering perfectionists, read on!

CHAPTER 8

Out of Control... into Happiness

L et's Get in the Mood for this chapter. Take a deep breath, close your eyes, and think of someone who drives you crazy. Think about the last time you felt out of control about a person, place, or thing. What situation has you constantly on edge and ready to lose it? Think of the last time you felt completely out of control. Who makes you want to pull your hair out? Okay now

CHECK ALL THAT APPLY

- ❑ I am so irritated!!!
- ❑ I can't take them anymore!
- ❑ What is wrong with people!!
- ❑ I can't believe he just did that!
- ❑ Why can't they see it? It's so logical! Are people blind? Stupid?
- ❑ I can't believe my daughter just did that...I did NOT raise her to be like that!
- ❑ Doesn't he know he's going to lose me if he doesn't stop drinking?
- ❑ I can't take her anymore!
- ❑ That's it, I'm done, you're dead to me.
- ❑ I can't stand the way he keeps doing that!
- ❑ I taught her better than that!
- ❑ I can't believe she is just throwing everything away after all I've done!

- ❑ Can't they see that it's wrong?! That they're wrong!
- ❑ If I could just get him to understand where I'm coming from he would change.
- ❑ Everything else is good except for that one thing that I keep hoping will change.
- ❑ I am sooooooo frustrated!
- ❑ Why aren't people more considerate?
- ❑ Why can't people be more realistic?
- ❑ I hate when people are inauthentic!
- ❑ I hate when people are disrespectful!!
- ❑ I am so tired of this!!
- ❑ What's WRONG with you??!!

Sound Familiar?

If you've checked more than half, I know how you feel. Control is definitely an illusion and is highly overrated!! Teachers think that if they are prepared enough, they can control their students. Parents think that if they are good enough parents, their kids will grow up with straight A's, A students, in A-list colleges, in A jobs and have A relationships. Employees think that if they do their job well they should get recognition and raises. Leaders think that if they are clear in their expectations, staff should be able to execute. Wives, husbands and partners think that if they are loving, if they are giving, if they keep their vows till death do us part, then the other will never leave, cheat, disrespect, and put the seat down!

Let Me Give You A "Peace" of My Mind

Marlene: "I fed you, bathed you, kept you healthy, paid for your schooling, gave you everything you asked for growing up, paid for the best college, and now you are going to throw it all away because you think you are smarter than me? That my beliefs are too old-fashioned and I know nothing? That you know better than me?! How dare you!! I just want you to be happy... how can you do this to yourself... how can you do this to me?"

For years, I would brag that my girls were not 'typical teens' as they were respectful, hard-working, straight-laced, and fine examples of what happens when you raise kids on gratitude and appreciation, and then, BOOM, it was over. One daughter made extremely poor choices that completely boggled my mind, and then a few years later my 'good daughter' began to express herself, and I didn't like what I was hearing!! I work with clients who are moms as well so I know I'm not alone! But the more I tried to 'control' my daughter, reason with her, cajole, bribe, threaten... nothing worked. I was in a constant state of irritation, frustration, and angst. We can cheat ourselves out of happiness when we try to unsuccessfully control partners, family members, coworkers, bosses and children.

> *Carol*: "What happened to the man who brought her flowers, who wrote her poems, who said in front of God and man that he would stay in good times and bad, rich and poor, till death did they part? I've been a good wife, cooked and cleaned and raised our kids, did my best to look my best, kept my end of the bargain even when I didn't feel like it... where did this addiction to alcohol and pot come from? I thought he had lost his job because of his unreasonable boss, but now I can no longer give him excuses. Can't he see that he's going to lose me and the family if he doesn't stop drinking? If I can just get him to see that there are many good reasons to make better choices he will stop. But I have and he hasn't. I am at my wit's end. I can't do this anymore."

Trying to control people we love so that they have better lives is one of the most difficult challenges my clients face. Watching their kids, partners, parents, employees spiral out of control in the clutches of addiction, irresponsible behavior, poor choices, self-mutilation, and self-sabotage is painful. So, they spend their own life blood, sweat, tears, and energy trying to help, but end up losing their own birthright to life happiness in the process. Am I saying that we should just not care? No, but if don't find balance, and use the airline recommendation to put on your own oxygen mask first before trying to help another, we might both go down in flames. Let's start with another Foundation Peace that will help you move you from feeling Out of Control into Happiness.

FOUNDATION PEACE: A Big Picture Look at Life and the Pursuit of Happiness

Why are we here? What is the meaning of life? What is the purpose of life? Are we happy? How do we define happiness? I love His Holiness the Dalai Lama's answer to the question, "What is the secret of Happiness?" "If I told you it wouldn't be a secret anymore!" Throughout each chapter, I've addressed different pieces of my Happiness Pie. Joy, Freedom, Forgiveness, Faith, Hope, Love, and Dignity are all big juicy slices of that pie. And the bottom line? Happiness is a CHOICE. And it all starts with what we choose to see as the map of life. Is our purpose to come into life at birth, grow up in a loving home, go to school, work hard, make money, buy nice things, have enough to retire in comfort, and die without too many bad things happening to us and those we love? If that is the expectation, then life becomes a fantasy. Since the majority of us grow up in unhealthy homes, and as I have mentioned before Oprah, my honorable moniker, says it's as high as 8 out of 10, the majority of us will have a false start immediately. No wonder so many of us are unhappy. Then, if there's loss of loved ones, health, jobs, homes, cars, money, or relationships, which there always is, it becomes progressively harder to be happy. One of the ways humans cope with loss is by trying to control people, places, and things. And the more we try to control our circumstances and people around us, the more uncontrollable things become, until we feel out of control and happiness is nowhere to be found.

What if life has nothing to do with status and comfort and being at the top of the heap? What if we don't have to control people places and things outside ourselves? What if life is supposed to be about experiencing joy, wonder, bliss, peace, kindness, and happiness most of the time? What if anger, sadness, and frustration some of the time is just for contrast? What if we are eternal spiritual beings from a place that is like heaven but that we get to come to earth and play and expand and experience the taste, touch, sound, feel, and smell of life? What if we line up like in an amusement park ride to come to earth to develop and grow different qualities like power or love or joy or beauty or kindness every time we're here? What if we come to earth to express our unique gifts, talents, and abilities in the environment we are born into, and if you are a Shirley MacLaine fan, we can do it more than once!

Then that would mean that everything that is happening to me, and to those I love, is happening for a reason, which I may not understand while it is happening. So, while my daughter seems to be throwing her future away, or while my husband is drinking himself to oblivion, or while my teenage daughter's friend is pot-smoking his way into home-lessness, I can choose to see Life as a JoyRide where in every circumstance I am developing and cultivating the quality that I came down to experience. I know this may sound very 'woo-woo' and super-Pollyanna, and my scientist readers will be demanding proof. I have no proof. But I do have proof in my life pudding!

Let Me Give You A "Peace" of My Heart

All I know is that for decades I lived in the unrealistic expectation that life was supposed to be a bed of roses, and that I was dealt a bad hand by God by being born into an abusive home, and that was NOT fair. I believed I was damaged goods, that I would never be able to 'catch up' to those who had perfect homes, that I would have to prove myself worthy and respectable for the rest of my accomplishment-driven life. That even when I was recognized for achievements, I would still feel unworthy, that I would think, "Wait till they figure out that I'm really not that great." With every recognition, it was never enough. I was not happy. I was choosing a BS story that was keeping me unhappy.

I was angry, bitter, in full-on resentment to my mother, and then to the 'wasband who cost me a half million dollars in a divorce settlement after he cheated with another pre-school mom. If life was about rolling with the punches, I was knocked out in five rounds. Again, I chose to feel hurt.

But because my secret life weapon is CHOICE, a concept I keep splattering over you chapter by chapter, and I took an 88 thousand foot look down at what life can mean, I can and do choose to believe that life is not random. I did not come to earth to just work hard and make money and die with toys. I came here as an eternal spiritual being to experience life and develop Power. What better way to cultivate Power than to be born in a home and choose relationships where I had no power. Yes, I took my out of control feeling over my painful past and my divorce and even my daughters and realized that the one thing I actually could control was the way I looked at what life was and could be. I feel so much happier choosing to believe that I came down into the perfect series of scenarios that help me become the Powerhouse that I want to be. Can you choose your happiness story?

What if life was about experiencing the entire spectrum of human emotion, of feeling, tasting, touching, smelling, and seeing all that is here for us on planet Earth, and even beyond? What if the painful pasts that we don't want to deal with are actually part of the plan? What if, by alchemizing and transforming through that pain, we come up with ways in which to help others through the same kind of pain? What if we're here to fulfill Emerson's definition of success: "To laugh often and much…to know that one life has breathed easier because we have lived?"

What if the very first thing we learn in life is that we are supposed to be happy, that we can be happy unconditionally, regardless of the conditions, and actually use the conditions to develop qualities and skills that will make our lives richer and even more fulfilled by serving others? What if happiness is not about growing up in a loving home, but that one can take any home and see the experiences from a different expansive perspective? What if work is not about making the most money in a job that I may not like but about fully expressing our creative gifts and making money in the process? What if happiness is not tied to how much material wealth we accumulate, but about how we can use the money to enhance our joy in helping ourselves and others? Not in a hedonistic, selfish, self-centered, hurtful-towards-self-and-others' way that is not joy, but in the self-care, self-expressed, fully creative way that is more than surviving through problems?

What if life isn't about making money, or controlling others using money, but about making peace, and creating wonder and bliss, first within our own hearts and minds, and then, by extension, with others. What if feeling happy 88% becomes the new currency that measures wealth? What if money can bring us a short-term high but we see that the long-term high is anchored in our new BS Belief System about our innate birthright to a limitless supply of wonder? What if even bad things that happen have a place in helping us grow and expand and develop and help and create and invent and aspire and inspire and learn and laugh and love? What if life is way more than just satisfying our desire for stuff and possessing each other? What if we learn that happiness and joy are our birthright, that peace and love are as important to us as the breath that fuels our heart? What if that feeling that comes when we love or are loved or bring love to another is exactly what the Universe intends for us when we come into this earth, and that all the things that happen to us help us expand toward that end? What if there is no other purpose for us than to live in-joy and en-joy? Once I use my secret weapon of CHOICE to choose a different way of looking at life I can take a giant step towards Happiness 88% of the time. I can then use some daily Balance tools to help build a stronger Happiness muscle.

Learning in Action with Balance Tools

☯ Balance Tool: A New Pair of Glasses when Life is Not Fair

So, what happened to you in the past that puts you in the damaged category? Mine was the childhood abuse by my mother, and then adult abuse by my 'wasband.' What's yours?

Take some time and write it out in full. By the way, if you'd like to do this or any other exercise with me, please get on my calendar and we'll go digging after damaged roots. If you get angry, don't stop. If you get sad, don't stop. Write it under the heading LIFE IS NOT FAIR.

_____

_____

_____

_____

Now use the same process that I did with my past. If I were a spiritual being having a human JoyRide experience, what did I want to develop being in the exact circumstance I was in? For me. I wanted to experience Power, so what better way to learn and expand into power than to be raised in a home and marriage of pure powerlessness? Take a breath and try to pan out and see your life as a Big Picture, with different filters than the one with which you grew up. Can you find the relief that comes with seeing that everything happens for a good reason? That you're not damaged goods, that pain is the touchstone of growth and expansion, that you are like a diamond, brilliant from the process of cutting and polishing? I can. With practice and your secret weapon of CHOICE you can, too.

Write a new narrative under the heading LIFE IS AN OPENING.

_____

_____

_____

_____

If you don't already feel relief from rewriting your past, you will. As your Balanced Centered Self gets stronger, he/she will know how to change from habits and mindsets that continue to keep us out of control and unhappy to new ones that will help us breathe easier.

☯ Balance Tool: The CORE of Who I Am

I have a friend who has not an answering machine but a questioning machine that says when you call, "WHO ARE YOU AND WHAT DO YOU WANT?" Answering the question, "Who am I?" helps paint yourself in the unique vibrant colors and patterns that you have become as a direct result of all of the painful experiences, rather than what you have seen yourself using the Life is not Fair pair of glasses.

Tapping into the wisdom of Balanced Center Self, we want to go back to any and all compliments that have ever been given to us, which you've already recorded in the Balance Tool Bake your own Cake Exercise back in Chapter 6: Fear to Freedom. And even if our Critic has responded with, "Well, you really aren't as good as they say you are, wait till they find out what you're really like!" or "You certainly have them fooled," or "You're not all that" your knowing of Who You Really Are will eventually soothe out the voice of the Critic. Happiness starts with an okay-ness about yourself, a self-love in your imperfectly perfect self, so let's start.

Intersect about eight lines so you have about 16 pieces of pie-shaped pieces. Now, start filling in adjectives that best describe You. You can tell your Critic to have a seat: "You must be tired, you've been working overtime all my life."

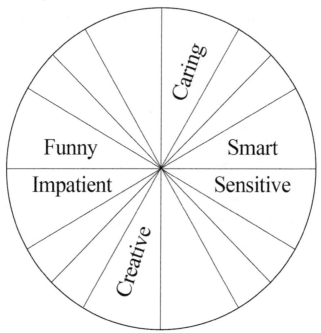

In my circle, I have the following parts of who I am: kind, self-sufficient, compassionate, lyrical, creative, ambitious, smart, attractive (even though my critic doesn't think so), funny (even though my wasband didn't think I was), critical, judgmental, impatient (all of which I swore I would never be because they were what my mother was), quick-learner, disciplined, sensitive (which is directly correlated to creativity so it's not a bad thing), and loving.

Don't let your critic fill in more than four negative descriptives, and if you're stuck, ask those who love you to help you fill in more positives. Owning your good qualities and loving yourself is not an automatic button you can push, especially if your Critic has been telling you otherwise all of your life. Be patient, and work to strengthen your Balance

Centered Self muscle and voice. Pin up your Core of Who I Am circle on your mirror and use it to backup your affirmations, if you have that practice. Now that you have a new pair of glasses, a Big Picture outlook, and a better understanding of the beauty that you are, you can work on being happier with some Balance tools when you can't control those around you.

☯ Balance Tool: Accept the Unacceptable

Christina: "I am so frustrated with my son. All he does is sit around and smoke pot. He's flunking his classes and gaining weight and I try to help him, but he won't listen. I don't know what to do?! This is not how loving sons behave!"

When people do rotten things that you know are good for them, you keep trying to change them or the situation, which continues to decrease your Happiness levels. If they are doing things to hurt themselves, and you can't stop them, it's hard to not want to control their behavior. "If they loved me, they wouldn't do that to me."

When you take a breath, sit back and say, "I accept the unacceptable," there is a bit of relief. It means I don't like it, I still don't like it, I really don't want it to be this way, but for my good health and happiness I accept it, because God knows nothing I have said or done has been able to change it. There is relief in waving the white flag of Acceptance. I have had countless experiences of my own and witnessed those of my clients with the magic that happens when we say, "I give." Many times, miracles occur that were not even in the realm of possible, like my mom apologizing to me for the abuse after not talking to me for eight years. We can continue to increase our happiness percentage by choosing to Accept the Unacceptable. What are some things that you have been trying to change unsuccessfully? Try putting them next to a White Flag of Acceptance:

I Accept that:

_____

_____

_____

_____

_____

_____

_____

_____

Another way to untangle oneself from control into the freedom of happiness that builds on acceptance is letting go of the handcuffs that come with expectations, realistic or otherwise.

☯ Balance Tool: Let My People Go!

In the 60's, there was a big movement to teach us to better communicate by using "I feel" statements as a way of promoting understanding, and, let's face it, as a way of manipulating behavior. It is all based on the premise that people make us feel angry, sad, mad, hurt. This assumption leads us to expectation hell, a belief that it is other people's jobs to make us happy. Don Miguel Ruiz whom I've had the honor of interviewing twice says it most colorfully: "We are all the lead actors in our drama of life. So, when we expect others to be our supporting actors we get in trouble. They are the lead actors in their own play!" So, when we think that it is our job to make others happy and that others have the job of making us happy, we start spinning out of control... there is no peace of mind, no peace of heart and definitely no happiness 88% of the time.

I practice what I preach most of the time, but no one can push my buttons better than my eldest daughter. I love her dearly, but, honestly, there is no one who can send me to the moon faster with some of the things she says and does... and her attitude! AND I know that if I stay in this place I will never get to happy 88% of the time. I have to let go of CONTROL. You and I have no control over another; we can have influence when the conditions are aligned, but control and forcing people to be supporting actors in the drama of our lives is completely crazy-making! So, when my buttons get pushed I say to myself, "**People do the very best that they can; if they could do better, they would. Right now, they can't. They are doing the very best that they can, and then I can let them go.**" This works for my interactions with my mother, and also to frame what my father did in contributing to the dysfunctional system with my mother. I don't think it's possible to completely be button-free until we die and return to the other side. But it is possible to shorten the time of discomfort after the initial ding-a-zing. Using the phrase, "She's doing the best that she can; if she could do better, she would," absolutely helps me restore my Peace of Mind when it comes to my teenage daughter! And I have to also qualify here, she is more than 88% fabulous now… a year away at college does miracles with gratitude!

Balance Tool: Don't Take it Personally

Rachel: "I don't understand why they don't like me…I haven't done anything to them but be nice. Now they are spreading gossip about me and it's just cruel."

When people are misbehaving, it is very difficult to be happy; it feels personal when people criticize you, blame you, violate you and your space, and trample all over your feelings. How could they say that? I haven't done anything to them… why would they attack me like that?! It makes no sense!" If you are also sensitive, these misbehaviors feel extra personal.

When toes get stepped on, my internal Brat will go on the offense and attack. My favorite bratty response is "If I looked like you, I'd look miserable, too!" Nope, not very nice, but my Brat, Agnes, loves it. And saying that might give me a minute of a reprieve, but eventually my Critic will start the rant of "See, you really are not all that and people hate you."

Choosing to say, 'It's not personal," even when it feels quite personal will keep you on the happier side of the street. Don Miguel Ruiz hits the nail right on the head with the 2nd agreement in his mega-bestselling book, *The Four Agreements "Don't take things personally"*. I also mentioned in the last chapter the *Fortune* magazine study that found the two biggest blocks to Leadership success: 1) Perfectionism and 2) Taking things too personally. And I want to be a leadership success… you?

Clyde: "My boss is a pain in my neck. He spits and screams at people when he's angry, and he takes credit for everyone's work. He is mean and cruel and his boss doesn't care. I would leave, but the money is really good and I don't want to lose out on this otherwise great job."

I may not be able to change my boss but I can decide that being mad at him every day at work is not a good use of my time or my emotions. So I choose not to take his flaws personally. Here's a practice exercise to help you react a little less out of control and not take things too personally whereby improving my own Happiness percentage.

Write down the name of people who irritate you and drive you to the moon, like Alice did Ralph in *The Honeymooners*. Beside their name, describe the behavior that make you lose control. In the third column, write down your old interpretation of why you think they did what they did to you. Let your Brat and your Critic help you fill in this piece. "Because they don't respect you, because they don't love you, because they're evil, because they are stupid, because they want to hurt you," could be some of the answers. Next, fill in a new column as your Balanced Centered Self using better feeling statements to soothe both the Brat and the Critic.

Name	Out of Control Behavior	How It Hurts Me	It's Not Personal

The bottom line? **"Everybody does the very best that they can... if they could do better they would, and they can't, so they don't. It's not Personal."**

☯ Balance Tool: Do You Want to Be Right or Be Happy?

An oldie but goodie...is it better to be right or be happy? If you're anything like the overachiever I am, you are saying, "I want both!" But the bottom line is that our happiness factor can be exponentialized when we release that insistent need to be right! Look at the times during the day when our irritation is fueled by that need. What would happen if we would just let things be exactly as they are? But, you protest, it's the principle! I can't just let this go; if I do then there's no right, there's no justice in the world! If I let everyone do whatever they very well please, aren't I doing them a dis-service...allowing them to do say and be whatever? And then I go for the extreme jugular; "Are you saying that I allow people to rape and kill and hurt people?" No, dear extremist, that's not what I'm saying. I am encouraging everyone who feels like they are constantly pissed off and angry and righteously indignant to consider not making a blanket statement, not go into turbo judgment mode and practice just letting go of control, because you CANNOT make people think, believe, say or do what you want them to! No matter how much it is logical, right, justified and "not how I raised you!" Can I just say "OK, you are right where you are?"

Tension, which will suck the happiness out of any interaction increases when I keep tension on my rope. When I release tension on my side of the rope, there is no tension. When I drop the rope, there is no longer a tug-of-war. You only have tension in a relationship when you insist on your side. And if you don't pick up the rope in the first place, tension can't touch you... and when there is no tension...there is no war... so LET GO OF THE ROPE! There is a wonderful feeling of relief when we cease fighting with anyone and everyone. Now, before you think I am advocating that you lay down and be a doormat or wall-to-wall carpet, I am not. You don't have to bow down. You can say, 'You are right' and then walk away. You can say 'That's an interesting way to look at it,' and walk away. You can say, 'I was hoping for something else so I'm going to hang up now,' and hang up. If there is bad behavior, they will have to suffer through their consequences and bump into themselves. But the way into happiness and out of control is to decide that IT IS NOT MY JOB TO MAKE THEM BUMP INTO THEMSELVES, especially when I might get hurt myself in the process. I think I just created a new fast to pair with my *21 Day Fast from Complaining with Dr. Marissa* called *21-Day Fast from Insisting that I'm Right* and see how that increases my happiness factor!

Time for a Balance Oath:

I, _____ (your name), do swear to try my best not to pick up the rope and get into an impossible, no-win, situation with _____ (their name) and just let them be right so I can be happy.

If you're having a hard time saying the oath, then go to the next Balance Tool.

☯ Balance Tool: Pearl-Makers

This tool is for advanced users and is the icing on the forgiveness cake that we baked in Chapter 5. Can I see the people places and things out of the same lens that my Unconditional Power Source/ UPS Man sees them? That's bringing in the big guns, choosing to believe that there is a much, much, much bigger picture that I cannot see if I keep trying to put my arms around and control. And, that if, indeed, we are taking a trip into this thing called Life, and that everything happens for our Divine and Best Good, even as we covered earlier, the painful experiences in our childhood (abuse, abandonment, neglect, loss, etc.) and in adulthood (betrayal, loss, abuse, tragedy, etc.), then we can see everything and every-one as an oyster sees a grain of sand. Because the sand irritates the oyster, it covers it up with layers and layers of a pearly substance that ends up, you guessed it, as a pearl! So, we can actually thank irritating people for helping us make pearls in life, like patience, tolerance, compassion, kindness, and love. So, instead of trying to control them, we can let them go and thank them, all the way into happiness 88% of the time!

Here are some additional Balance mantras to help reinforce the movement from Out of Control into Happiness.

☯ Balance Tool: Alphabet Soup for Happiness

I've developed a number of acronyms that help me soothe my Critic when it is either jumping up and down amplifying feedback from others, and my Brat who wants to fight back, so that I can have fun loving relationships. They are great ammunition for the Balanced Centered Self to restore Happiness.

INTBOAD: It's Not That Big Of A Deal!

When I am incensed with someone or something that isn't unfolding perfectly I use INTBOAD, because it's the truth! Once I've had time to step back and look at the person, place, thing or situation from a broader 88-thousand-foot view or perspective, I can see that in the global scheme of things, knowing that I live in a Friendly Universe and choosing to know that everything is always working out for me, it really is not that big of a deal that the person is not cooperating, or saying mean things about me, or not meeting deadlines. The other part of this Balance mantra is proof in the memory pudding. When I try to remember back to what was eating me alive last week, or when the world was going to end the month before... I have a difficult remembering what it was... simply because INTBOAD!

IJM It's Just Money

I hate losing money. Forgetting to use a money-saving coupon can drive me batty... even when it's only one dollar. I can blame it on my Chinese heritage and/or on my perfectionism. Regardless of the underpinnings, I can launch myself from perfectionism into joy with this simple statement. Again, I know that it will make me feel better to let go of the angst from something that wasn't perfect and may have cost me money. I actually love the story of a man who went to his bosses' office after losing a 2 million dollar deal. Fully expecting to be fired, he was stunned when his boss said, "Now why would I fire you when I just spent two million dollars educating you?" Now the balance is that we don't want to keep learning the same lesson over and over again and lose our shirt, pants and underwear endlessly, but most perfectionists I know do sweat the small stuff, especially myself, so we can let this one go so Joy will come easier.

ICBW: It Could Be Worse

When we are brooding that things didn't go our way, or someone or something didn't happen the way we wanted it to, this Balance mantra helps put perspective on our perfectionistic pissing contest. When my clients start wallowing in their "poor me" too long, I send them to YouTube to watch "No arms, no legs, no worries" Nick Vujicic who easily embodies that ICBW… it always could be worse…so put on your big girl panties and move on!! By the way, I've never met anyone who has more of a right to be unhappy and gives up that right and not only chooses happiness but is also using his unique perspective to inspire the world. I hope to have him on my show one day.

TTSP: This, Too, Shall Pass

I love these words…I use it so much that I can almost deactivate any irritating angst I am feeling. For me, it triggers words from Eckhart Tolle, another one of my life teachers who says that there are three magical words that are the key to happiness… ONE WITH LIFE. If we can be okay with whatever happens to us, good, bad, and ugly, then we have topped ourselves with an unlimited supply of happiness.

☯ Balance Tool: The 21-Day Fast from Complaining with Dr. Marissa

The last tool I am going to soft blanket you with is the 21 Day Fast from Complaining with Dr. Marissa Pei, a diet and exercise program for your mind, soul and spirit. As I shared earlier in the Law of Attraction Foundation Peace, what you focus on will expand. So, if you are spewing complaints and negativity, you will attract more people places and things to complain about. Edwene Gaines, a great speaker and teacher, came to Agape International Spiritual Center in 2011 and said that if you did not complain for 21 days, you would attain spiritual ascendance. And since I love a challenge and love competition, I started the fast on July 1st, 2011 online. And since research says it takes 21 days to break a bad habit and create a good habit, and good habits are meant to be shared and continued, I am currently on Round 80, where I post Balance Tips on a daily basis on how to stay complaint-free. So, this is one exception to my perfection rule...you can strive to be complaint free for 21 days and do it perfectly! I've added videos, motivational cards and now an APP with Balance tips every morning for 21 days to help you say when asked, "How are you?" with a smile, " No Complaints!" There is a Warning Label for the Fast... it may be hazardous to anxiety, worry, hostility, anger or overall grumpiness. And after 18 days, side effects may include increased smiling, laughing out loud, improved mood and relief from Mean-o-Pause (formerly known as Menopause) and the male counterpart IMS (Irritable Man Syndrome). So please do join me on Facebook and give me the finger at Dr. Marissa...I mean a thumbs up so we can continue 8 ways to Happiness together using the Balance Tool of No Complaints!

Breathe. Smile and Relax.

Next, we call it a wrap in the conclusion...

In Conclusion: Phoenix Rising

I hope you have had as much fun reading and working through this Happiness Handbook as I have had writing it, or more accurately stated, having it written through me. I have laughed, aha'd at myself, cried, blushed, and said "Did I really write that down out loud?!"

I hope that you had a good laugh at the Labyrinth of Shiitake, my Pregnancy Model of Relationships, and the myriad of Balance mantras and tools that I want you to use to shovel out all of your past pain and future fear Shiitake which are great to use as fertilizer in growing the beautiful you. And if you are a skimmer, please go back and do the exercises. They only work when you do them! I know the perfectionists already have... ha!

I hope that through reading this book you can see past pain in a new way, as a touchstone to transformation and expansion for our mind and soul. We all alchemize, purity from the fire of life, and rise from the ashes into the phoenix of our lives. What if that is the true role of pain? What if every tragedy, from loss to heartbreak to shame to hatred to loneliness to loss of control, is the touchstone with which our hearts are broken wide open to then champion that very cause, so that the entire planet would benefit from our healing light? What if every wrong was supposed to exist to give us a chance to stand and love and heal and rise again to make it right? What if that is what life is all about -- not to suffer from the tragedies but to create hotspots that fuse connections towards a common solution to the humankind condition? Wouldn't that be an awesome truth for us all to choose? And surprise, but no surprise, my middle name in Chinese is "Fung," which means Phoenix.

I hope that you have allowed your Balanced Centered Self to expand, strengthen, disinfect and bless the blocks that the Critic, Brat and Sad One have used to protect themselves, so that all the shiitake can now be shoveled back in as fertilizer, to grow the beauty that is uniquely you. And if you don't see yourself that way yet, that's okay, I will hold and support you in that Truth until you do. Because I know that we can all rise above anything and everything that is standing in our way of our birthright in life…to be loving lovable and loved. So, fall back into my Friendly Universe… until you can see yours too.

I hope that you have above all, a little sparkle of Hope in your Heart and a little less Muck in your Mind. I hope that you understand why and how and what is going on that keeps you singing the chipmunk song "I'm Lonely,", Suffering in Loss, Sinking in Shame, Drowning in Heartache, Marinating in Hatred, Paralyzed in Fear, Stuck in the Box of Perfectionism, and totally Out of Control. But, most importantly, I hope you have allowed me to give you a Peace of my Mind and my Heart so that you have a way out of Loneliness into Hope, out of Loss into Faith, out of Heartbreak into Love, out of Hatred into Forgiveness, out of Shame into Dignity, out of Fear into Freedom, out of Perfectionism into Joy and out of Control into Happiness… 88% of the time. Because you're worth it!

Acknowledgements

I have written this transcript of my life because of my incredible love affair with my UPS Man, my Universal Power Source who I plug into every day when I meditate.... Who blesses me with so much love it brings tears just knowing how much I am wrapped in a warm blanket of worthiness. It started that Sunday February 22nd when He tapped me on the shoulder and said "Darling, you can church shop all you want, have fun with it, but know that I've always been here waiting for you to turn around and Dance with Me." My success on the air and on paper is because I say "Speak/write through me, don't let me get in the way...let the Words be Thine and the voice be mine." I get to be a Light connected to a Power Source that conspires for and never against me. Breathe. Smile. Love.

Then there is my big brother, Dr. Michael Bernard Beckwith, who gave me the key to unlock my heart from the basement of bitterness and showed me who I really am in the glory of who I am, who saw into me more than I could ever imagine and continues to hold me in that Truth.

To my mom Rose and my daughters Chloe Mei and Sarah Wei who carry the light of my inheritance of the Tao women, the strength, the beauty and the power of possibility...along with the imperfection that keeps me humble and expanding into more and more good.

To Dolores and Graham Martin, my other mom and dad, whose daily connection keeps me right-sized and reminded of how loved and supported I am in a design for living for me that is Happy Joyous and Free.

To Mary Richardson, my constant abiding life reminder that I am never alone, and that things will always change and that I will not be in pain forever.

To Karen Stuth my editor, whose dream about this book's future gave it a booster shot.

To David Hancock and his team at Morgan James Publishing who expanded the booster shot into a slingshot into the literary world of wonder.

To Cory Bowden, whose brilliant technical expertise makes me look good on-line and off-line!

To all of my teachers, friends, supporters, listeners, virtual connections who give me the finger/thumbs up every day and even the people who have helped me make pearls…you know who you are!

Yes, thanks to all who anchor me in the knowing that I am Loving, Lovable, and Loved.

Shea Shea.

About the Author

Introducing Marissa Pei, Ph.D. an Inspirational Speaker lecturing and teaching world-
wide on Life Balance Hope and How to be Happy 88% of the time, TV Commentator on Discovery and Learning Channel specials, ABC, FOX and KTLA/KUSI/CW6 on Relationships, Tragedy and Hope, On-Air Personality with a popular award-winning talk radio/TV show in its 6th year called *"Take My Advice, I'm Not Using It: Get Balanced with Dr. Marissa"* on the Universal Broadcasting Network out of the Sunset Gower Studios in Hollywood, syndicated on CNBC News Radio KCAA AM1050 FM102.3 FM106.5 and syndicated nationally on IHeartRadio. Her honorable moniker 'the Asian Oprah' began because of many past Oprah guests on her show along with winning the 2014 Asian Heritage Award, Business Person of the Year Lotus Award and the 2012 Asian

Entrepreneur of the Year Award. Her awards continue with the 2016 Top 10 Podcast of the Year Award from a field of 440 thousand shows and 100 million downloads, and is included on the OC500 List of the most Influential People from a field of 3.5 million in Orange County California. Her most recent award 2017 Iconic Women Creating a Better World for All was received while speaking at the Women's Economic Forum in India. Her celebrity media role now garners her invitations to cover Red Carpets and has interviewed Halle Berry, John Travolta, Priscilla Presley, Fran Drescher and Quincy Jones to name a few. Dr. Marissa moonlights as a broadcast journalist and columnist with articles in the OC Register, The Sun Newspaper. Forbes and Inc. magazines have published features about her, highlighting her expertise in Human Dynamics at Work, Interpersonal Effectiveness and PR/Branding. In the corporate world, using her doctorate in Organizational Psychology, Dr. Marissa works as a Consulting Psychologist for Fortune 500 companies like Johnson & Johnson, Wells Fargo, Cedars-Sinai, AT&T, Mattel, Toyota & Bank of America for the past 25+ years helping organizations improve Leadership Development/Executive Coaching, Strategic Planning, Teamwork, Valuing Diversity -- all culminating in More Joy, Less Stress and More Success at Work. She is a Life Balance Coach, Balance Tai Qi Qong creator and instructor, meditation teacher, singer/songwriter, and a retired professor teaching at the Anderson Graduate School of Management UCLA, Boston University Brussels and European Business School. Dr. Marissa is recognized as a Global Thought Leader with her 21 Day Fast from Complaining and Peacework around the Planet. Finally, Dr. Marissa races sailboats and raises 2 girls as a single mom for fun. Her life mottos are 'No Regrets' for the past and 'Don't Die Wondering!' for the future…because the Present is a Gift, so Unwrap it!

Morgan James
Speakers Group

www.TheMorganJamesSpeakersGroup.com

We connect Morgan James published authors with live and online events and audiences who will benefit from their expertise.